THE VISITOR

A Near-Death Covid Experience Taught One Man
Faith, Prayer, Love, and Charity are
God's Remedies to Survive and Thrive

Sean Kelley

En Route Books & Media, LLC
Saint Louis, MO

En Route Books and Media, LLC
5705 Rhodes Avenue
St. Louis, MO 63109

Cover credit: Chas Kelly

Copyright © 2022 Sean Kelley

ISBN-13: 978-1-956715-48-4
Library of Congress Control Number: 2022937584

No part of this book may be reproduced, stored in a retrieval system, or transmitted in any form, or by any means, electronic, mechanical, photocopying, or otherwise, without the prior written permission of the author. No adaptation or group use for training or repackaging may be done without the express written authorization of the author.

Visit us online at https://enroutebooksandmedia.com/thevisitor/

I dedicate this to all the life-saving nurses, doctors, husbands, and wives that have battled or are currently battling COVID and any other terminal illness. May you keep the faith as you struggle through this adversity.

A portion of the sales proceeds will be given to the non-profit, Cards for Covid. Please visit www.cards4covid.org to check out the mission.

Acknowledgments

First, EVERYONE who has said a prayer for me along the way, I have felt your prayers and I am ALIVE because of them! THANK YOU!

My wife, Monica Saller Kelley, for channeling the Archangel Michael and going to battle against the COVID in our home, and for taking the steps to get me the lifesaving treatments prior to going to the hospital. I love you for what you do and more so for who you are.

Jaime Matthiesen Cheaney, for working with Monica to help me get the life-giving care that kept me alive before going to the hospital. You are a true Saint, and I am forever grateful for the love you and your Heather Cheaney poured out for me! I love you both.

To Lisa Saller, Rachel Preiss Genovese, Mary Saller, Andrea DeMarco Lopes and so many other amazing women that provided emotional support, love, and guidance for my wife. Your love for my wife was awe-inspiring and I am forever grateful.

To Matt Saller and Kristen Saller for taking Emma for a few days so she could spend time with her cousins, lift her spirits, and give my household more peace as I heal through this.

Beatrix Mohsenin, there hasn't been a day gone by that you haven't said a prayer for me. You are a true friend and a wonderful human being. Thanks for filling my heart with faith to help me prepare for this battle and being my prayer Warrior throughout it! I am blessed to have you in my life!

 Tom Agresti, Monica Sauceda Agresti, and Cece Agresti… Cece's prayers and videos are SO sweet! Monica's attitude is SO positive! Thank you for being a true friend, for sending my wife and I life-saving information, and for ALWAYS supporting me through thick and thin. Tom, you are an amazing human being!

 To Lynn Piontek Schroeder, Jim Whitesides, April Moeckel, the Stuckameyers, and ALL the rest of my neighbors, thank you for all the love, prayers, and meals! When we moved into this neighborhood, I had no idea how much love, care, and deep relationships we would get to experience with all of you.

 Justin Dumas, and anyone else who has sent food to the nurses at the Mercy South 6 Medical Stepdown COVID Unit. I am grateful for you to help those who saved my life, those heroes are exalted by you and that is my greatest reward from all of this.

 Reid V Richards, each morning before dawn when you send me videos of your beautiful son, you bring the sunrise. Thank you for bringing so much knowledge and light to the world!

 The Car Motivators team members; Aimee Smith, Chas Kelly, and Nikhil Sachdeva, for springing into action by updating our coaching clients consistently. Taking on ALL the workload, ensuring all tasks were done and coaching just like I would, or BETTER! I LOVE you guys with ALL my heart, and I am SO blessed to have you in my life. We'll be taking that trip sooner than you can imagine 😊

Acknowledgments

Fellow Automotive Professionals Frank J Lopes, Rebecca Chernek, Ted Ings, Jonathan Dawson, Bart Templeton, Chris Scott, Jason Volny, Laurie Foster, Velko Tuhchiev', Lisa Copeland, and more... Your prayers, support, and encouragement through this have been nothing short of a miracle. Thank you for propping me up, sharing my messages, and for being downright AMAZING people! I love YOU for your hearts, your leadership, and the light you bring my beloved automotive industry!

Trev Oliver and Garrett Caldwell, your video making fun of me brought me so much joy and laughter! And even though it sent me into a hypoxic episode... it was SO worth it! Haha

Michelle Marie Sri, your prayers impacted me. You have the endurance of Job, and watching your story of what you've been through with your cancer, I found your experience gave me strength and continues to do so as I heal. Your brutal journey has made mine a cake walk and for that, I thank you!

Deacon Steven M Schisler, for bringing me into Catholicism like a champion Deacon, for being one of my greatest mentors in faith and for always being here for my family and me. I love you Deacon Steve, and your beautiful wife Debbie!

The entire Jeff Wood and Tanner Wood family, for their unyielding love, the beautiful lessons they teach me, the love they have for each other, and for always being there for me.

Donald Brown, Brian Dorsett, Jason Bahr, Tom Agresti for joining the board of the new non-profit we're launching called Cards4COVID.org check out our website! We're going to do GODS WORK! This is WHY God gave me this blessing of

COVID, so we can move forward and make THIS impact on the world!

John Sevier, for inspiring me to post about deeper subjects than just "selling cars," which led me to meeting Brittany Hibdon, whose spirit brought me back from the brink of death. And to John's beautiful family for all their prayers and support. I love those precious kids of yours!!!

Brian Leach and Cate Leach, two amazing people with righteous faith and unwavering love, for creating one of the most joy-filled loving humans I have ever met while on this earth, Brittany Hibdon. And the woman who passed on in September, Brittany Hibdon. Brittany, though your body is gone, we now know you are watching over us, keeping us safe. We love you!

ALL my clients for your continued support and partnership through all this, you guys are my greatest motivation. Seeing you and your people develop, grow, and achieve more in business and life is my WHY. Thank you for allowing me to live my life's purpose through your team. I LOVE YOU #MOTIVATORS

ALL the medical professionals at Mercy Hospital South, you guys are the ultimate GIFT to the world. You fight strong and tirelessly, you sacrifice for others, your knowledge is deep, your cause is pure. I am with YOU! My family and friends are WITH YOU! God is WITH YOU! You WILL be Exalted!!! To this you have my word.

Brian Dorsett, for his faith mentorship, prayers, and for sending me the most beautiful gospel music that helped me remain at peace through some serious physical pain.

Acknowledgments

Sam Cavett, for inspiring me to "Win the battle in the mightiest of ways!" Inspired me to do so much more than just "get well" while in the hospital.

Paul Sansone, Jr., for forcing me to turn off my phone and sleep, knowing I need to recover. My wife and mother are forever grateful to you. Paul called me and said, "Sean, I know you want to save the world, and you're going to, but now you need REST. So, rest now or you're FIRED!" I love you man! ☺

My children, for their unconditional love, faith I would make it, and care they've given me since my return home. Truly among Jack, Ava, and Emma, I have a team of Nurses bringing me anything and everything I need on a whim. I am SO blessed to have you in my life!

To my Mother Barbara Stelmar. Mom, you have borne a heavy burden your entire life. God wants you to spend your remaining years enjoying the love of your family. I completely forgive you and love you for everything you are. Thank you for showing me that even in your 70s you can have the energy to take care of a sick son, be open to personal growth, let go of judgment, accept painful words while remaining introspective and evolve as a person. You are truly my inspiration! Thank you for helping make me who I am today.

Joel Rutherford, for his leadership, friendship and for making me a better human being while in Iraq which helped prepare me for this battle.

Keith Rosen, coach. Even though you've had eye surgery and have been in great pain of late, you've been there to support me, read my texts, reply to me, and uplift me through my darkest times. You taught me everything about coaching! Thank you for all your wisdom, support, and guidance. You mean the world to me!

Chad B. Carden, for being the ultimate mentor. When I was struggling to find my way, you helped me with a clear path. You taught me candor, something that was missing in my life. I have used this power to help countless individuals including myself and my own family. You have impacted the lives of so many, I can't thank you enough for your inspirational messages and love throughout this time, and my life before COVID.

David Fultz and DriveCentric CRM team for all your powerful prayers since I've been sick and the support you've given me through the years. I love you guys with ALL my heart!

Nikhil Sachdeva and Richa for springing into action for Cards4COVID.org website, for the temple prayers in India and for being all-around amazing human beings. You guys amaze me, fill me with joy, and I am so glad to have you in my life and business.

Brittany Zeller and Michael Zeller for the delicious cookies, we love them so much!

Jay and Amy Alexander, thank you for the prayers, support, and chicken soup. It warmed my family's heart during this cold dark time in our lives!

Thanks to Jennifer and Eric Olson for their hilarious video (Eric interview!) 😄, for being such fun and awesome friends and such amazing gunsmiths, and for the get-well ice cream cake, and of course for the timely introduction to my book publisher! Your family is a true pleasure to be around, and you always lift our spirits!

Bill Schomburg for your righteous faith, your unconditional love for all of us, the strength exemplified after losing your wife, and the long-term friendship you and your amazing brother, John Schomburg, have given me!!!

Rich and the paramedics at Rock Township Ambulance District, for safely transporting me to the hospital and getting here so quickly when I was in distress!

Thanks to Mary at The Blue Owl for making the most delicious and beautiful cake for my doctors and nurses up at Mercy!

Jason Gerasimovich, for all your hilarious videos, posting a prayer request for me on LinkedIn and for that amazing uplifting attitude of yours! Love you brother!

Table of Contents

Acknowledgments i
Introduction..1
Ch. 1: Tragedy Can Strike Without Warning........................7
Ch. 2: How Stubbornness Nearly Got Me Killed................15
Ch. 3: The Lowest Moment...27
Ch. 4: Miracles 35
Ch. 5: Fear the Disease, Not the Cure 43
Ch. 6: The Power of Prayer and Love..................................49
Ch. 7: It is Always Darkest Just Before the Dawn..............59
Ch. 8: God's Plan...69
Ch. 9: Here Comes the Sun..75
Ch. 10: Healing the Whole Person 81
Ch. 11: The Endurance of Job 91
Ch. 12: Coming Back to Life 97
Ch. 13: Another Epidemic: Unrealistic Self-Expectation.....109
Ch. 14: Spiritual Warfare: We Wrestle Not with Flesh and
        Blood 133
Appendix I 149
Appendix II 165
Appendix III 169

Introduction

Nearly dying due to COVID was the best thing that ever happened to me. That might sound like a crazy thing to say, but let me explain.

Before my near-death experience, and the many months of illness and healing afterward, I was a stressed out, fearful, guilt-ridden, resentful man. Yes, I was successful from the outside looking in. Owning my own thriving company in the people development and executive coaching world. Overall, I was doing work that I enjoyed, but I felt stuck in business and in life.

Out of fear of losing business, I would do all the work myself so it could be done perfectly. Trusting my team to do things was like trying to pry something from an alligator's mouth. Because I grew up extremely poor, I was fearful of losing money and being poor again. As a result, I wouldn't invest it like I needed to back into the people on my team who were so diligently helping me build my business. Fear of not being liked or being seen as a loser caused me to waste money on cool toys that became insignificant and uninteresting to others after the first five-minute "cool shock factor" wore off.

With all the things on my plate that I refused to give up and delegate out to my team, I didn't have time for anything else but owning, managing, accounting for, marketing, selling, and working in my business. I didn't leave enough room in my life for faith. I didn't leave enough energy in my body for a lot of meaningful time with my amazing wife, Monica, my son Jack, and my daughters Ava and Emma. This lack of faith and family time led to a lot of guilt.

So, I would throw money and gifts at them, instead of giving them what they really needed. Me. In addition to feeling guilt for having no time to spend with my family, I felt guilty for having money. My six brothers and sisters and I grew up extremely poor. Poor to the point where we were homeless for a year after a house fire. Poor people who have nothing often spend time resenting the rich people who have money. As a successful entrepreneur who generates great income, I felt guilty about my income. This would cause me to squander it on useless things or trips so I could make myself poor again and not feel, deep down hidden within me, shame for having money. Instead of tithing at my church, there's that lack of faith again, I might spend it on an expensive trip or a bigger home. Instead of donating to a cause I care about, like cancer, veterans, children, poverty, etc., I might buy another car instead.

Before this experience, I harbored a lot of resentment. I resented my mother for "vanishing" for two years when I was growing up when she was put into a psychiatric ward for manic depression and dissociative personality disorder. I resented my mother for the strife that I allowed to happen between her and my wife, which I always ended up hearing about from my bride. This caused me to avoid my mother at all costs, and, of course, resent my wife for telling me about it and not just "dealing with it." I resented my father for all the divorces he had put me and my siblings through (even though we wouldn't have existed without all the divorces!) Because I was holding onto all these resentments, if I ever felt slighted or disrespected by someone, I would harbor those resentments, too. Instead of communicating issues like an adult, I would avoid the discomfort a difficult conversation would cause all together.

Before almost dying on December 18th, 2021, I could see with my eyes, but I was blind to the fact that I was wasting my life acting out of fear, missing opportunities to live as a true Christian because of guilt, and destroying my relationships with resentment. Can you relate to any of these fears, guilts, or resentments?

Everything changed thanks to my near-death experience, being touched by a loving spirit who performed a miracle to save my life, and feeling the warm embrace of God. These helped me realize and internalize that our life is a brief and precious gift. It is a gift from our Father that must not be squandered focusing solely on worldly possessions and trivial matters. When it's our time to leave this earth, we are gone in an instant, sometimes with no time to prepare. It is so important to see every mundane interaction as an opportunity given by God to make a positive impact. I learned that we can never miss a chance to make a positive impact on our fellow humans because we are one body.

This near-death experience has given me a powerful blessing in that I was able to see the legacy I would have left behind had I been called home. As a result of my short 40 years of life, and my time in business as a leadership and sales coach, there were hundreds of people I have been blessed to meet and work with. These people were praying for me, thanking me for the impact on their lives, sending me soup to heal, while calling and messaging my wife and I throughout the entire healing process.

Before this experience, I thought much less about my legacy and the long-term impact, and my focus was more on growing a business. Now, I understand that the only thing that really matters in life is that we do what is right and just in the eyes of our Lord. Bringing His kingdom of love, light, hope, faith, and family to earth is the most important thing.

Thanks to God bringing me to my knees, I was able to trust my team after seeing them step up and lead my business to succeed without me. I was able to trust almost all of my clients, in seeing them rally around me, pray for me, work with my team members, and show me how much they love working together. I now know I will never go hungry again as long as I continue to bring value to them. God will always provide if you always walk in His path. I now harbor no resentment for anyone in my family, or any other human being on this earth. Thanks to my brush with death and God's touch, all the fear, shame, and guilt I used to have are completely gone.

In reading this book, what I want for you is inspiration, clarity, and freedom. I want you to have the same clarity and understanding from my experience, and internalize the same lessons, that I did, but without enduring the pain and months of healing required. I want to inspire you to live the most fulfilling life possible that truly opens the gateway to heaven for you and your family, while allowing you to feel fulfilled while on this earth. I want for you to have clarity around what it takes to heal both your soul and your body as you or your family battle COVID or any other potentially terminal illness. Also, I want for you to have freedom from your fear, guilt, and resentments that are holding your worldly success back and preventing you from achieving true internal happiness. If you want those things for yourself, then read on, this book is for you.

One more note, please don't look at this book as coming from just one guy who recovered from almost dying of COVID talking to you. The writings in this book come from over one hundred interviews with extremely talented Doctors, Nurses and severe COVID survivors, hundreds of hours of studying scripture, years of coaching some of the most successful leaders on the planet, speaking with religious mentors, and prayer. All these people have lent their voice to this book. God, Himself, is speaking as well.

The lessons in this book come from God's perfect plan for myself and my family, executed flawlessly. God seldom speaks to us directly with His voice; it's almost always through our experiences, and other people.

Remember this, God is always trying to get through to you. The question is, what are you hearing? How are you taking His instruction and changing? If you can't answer these questions clearly, read on, because this book is for you.

Finally, throughout this book, there are QR codes that will allow you to view my near-death journey firsthand with the photos and videos I've documented. If you want to be closer to my trip, use the camera app on your smartphone, and scan them to open the website. Some of the images are graphic photos of my health decline and may not suit all audiences. In addition, some of the videos are incredibly emotional; please view them at your own risk.

Chapter 1

Tragedy Can Strike Without Warning

Human beings are planners. We always are thinking about what we're going to do next week or next month or next year. We look forward to the next holiday, dream, and plan out events like weddings, parties, and vacations. We even schedule meetings, sometimes months in advance. We like to plan, and often assume everything will go according to *our* plan. The truth is our plans aren't important, because, ultimately, they can be disrupted in the blink of an eye by forces beyond our control.

My Plans with My Friend and Client

It was Friday, September 17, 2021, and I exchanged a series of texts with Brittany Hibdon, a client of mine who was also a good friend.

> *Brittany: Sean, there are 6 more team members that need to complete the cultural assessment survey for our dealership. Hopefully, we can get that done and review their answers while you're here!*
>
> *Sean: We can make that happen! I can't wait to coach with you and the team in person again!*

What time do you want me there Monday morning?

Brittany: Let's get started early say 7 am. That way you can coach the service team first thing after the morning service rush. We've had so many wins in the past year, we're excited to see you too! Can you jump on a call later?"

Sean: Sure! Call me after 4:30 pm.

During our conversation, we walked through the schedule and agenda for our visit. Brittany mentioned she, her husband, Shawn, and their two beautiful sons, Westly and Houston, all wanted to take me to dinner Tuesday night. I couldn't have been more excited to spend time with my friends, clients, and their families. Great plans.

As I boarded my Southwest flight on Sunday the 19th to fly to northern California, I had no clue what was really in store for me that week. The plan was to show up at Hibdon Auto Center, coach with Brittany the Dealer Principal, then spend the rest of the day coaching with each person on her team to help them sell more cars, increase profits in service and sales, and work to improve the overall communication, team cohesion, and culture of the dealership.

Brittany and I had been working together since February 2019 when she saw a LinkedIn post I had made about a manager who was dealing with a suicidal employee. After coaching with that manager on how to help their employee find help, a colleague and friend named John Sevier told me posting stories like that would help me connect with the right clients for my business. It worked, as it led me to meet one of the best leaders and most rewarding coaching relationships in my professional career to date, Brittany Hibdon.

She replied to my post, "Timely post, thank you."

I sent her a personalized video asking her, "I'm glad my post helped! May I ask, how was this timely for you? What can I do to help you with your situation?"

She explained she had an employee whose drinking was affecting their work, and my post helped her realize that she needed to find him professional help. Which she did.

One thing led to another, and from February 2019 to September 2021, we worked together each month. I would visit them annually, and coach with her team monthly. Brittany and I would coach at least once a week. She was a true leader with empathy, a growth mindset, and a passion for watching others succeed in life. For more about Brittany's leadership style, please check out my blog about her at www.carmotivators.com/blog

Over the course of those two-and-a-half years, Brittany was never late for a coaching conversation, and she never canceled one of our meetings. That's why when I arrived at her dealership the morning of September 20th and her husband said, "It's just going to be you, me, and the team today, Brittany is out sick." I was very surprised.

After all, once Brittany had wanted to coach when she had strep throat! I thought to myself, "She must be *very* sick to miss out on our annual coaching visit."

Regardless, we proceeded to accomplish the mission and dove into our coaching day. About 2:00 p.m. I was coaching with Brittany's husband, Shawn Hibdon, and he received a text from Brittany.

Get home now.

"I apologize, but Brittany needs me home. Can you finish up with the team?" he asked with concern for his family in his eyes.

"Of course, I can. Please go take care of Brittany. We've got this under control here!" I replied, trying to comfort him about his business. The managers and I had such a good relationship I knew we would knock it out of the park.

The plan was to do just that, and then I could celebrate with Brittany and Shawn. If she felt better, we would go out to dinner Tuesday night. That worked for my plans since I was going to be in town coaching the dealership of Brittany's great friend, Brenna Stransberry, at Park Marina Motors. Then I would fly out Wednesday to work with a Mercedes dealership in Nashville, TN.

Early the next morning I woke to my phone ringing. There was a voicemail before I could get to it. Ron the Hibdon Auto Center office manager had left me a very concerning voicemail. This man was a professional accountant and business controller. He was normally not the emotional type, but in his voice I heard great sadness, and I could tell he was shaken up.

I called him back to find out that Brittany Hibdon died Monday night in her home while waiting for the ambulance to arrive. Upon meeting Shawn, her absolutely distraught husband, I listened as he shared the details of what happened.

"Brittany's breathing was very shallow. I kept trying to calm her down. She kept saying, 'No hospital, no ventilator. No hospital, no ventilator.' But I told her, 'If you can't get your breathing under control, I will have to call an ambulance.'" He paused and continued to cry for a few minutes.

Shawn composed himself and continued, "She was shallow breathing so I flipped on the light, and I couldn't believe what I saw… she was ghost white, her lips were purple, and her pupils were dilated. Immediately, I picked up the phone and called 911… The operator had me timing Brittany's breaths, and she told me to say 'now' every breath, and at first it was like this."

He rapidly said "now" every second, "Now, now, now, now." Then he gradually slowed the "nows" to every 3 seconds, then 5 seconds, then he stopped.

"I saw her take her last breath." He burst into tears again. I hugged him tight.

He continued the story, "The operator told me to give her CPR, and she counted with me. At some point we were in the eighties, and I lost count. And she said, 'That's okay, just start over at one.' It was almost thirty minutes before the ambulance arrived."

"They worked on her for quite some time and took her to the hospital and worked more there to save her, but pronounced her dead after an hour. Now, we have to figure out a way to move forward without her." Shawn was clearly devastated.

I canceled my flight home, canceled the rest of my coaching projects for the week, and stayed there to help her family and team pick up the pieces. Meeting with Brenna and sharing the horrific news with her was one of the hardest things I've ever done in my life. She and I spent the day working together, because that's what Brittany would want, and crying together because we were so distraught. This was not part of my plan.

LESSON LEARNED

<u>Be Trusting</u>

It's great and even virtuous to plan because that's how we continuously improve and eventually achieve goals. One of my favorite quotes comes from the great and late Zig Ziglar. "If you fail to plan, you are planning to fail."

All that being said, planning needs to come with some degree of humility, and understanding that God's plan will always supersede our own. In life, tragedy will strike. There will be turmoil, loss, pain, and suffering. It's no different than how God suffered in the loss of his only son, Jesus Christ.

When planning, ask God to make it so your plan aligns to His will. When things don't go your way, it can be extremely painful, but rest assured that these painful moments are part of God's design. This design will have positive affects in your life

Chapter 1: Tragedy Can Strike Without Warning

or even the lives of others if you watch for them long after the painful moment occurs.

KEY SCRIPTURE

"Can any one of you by worrying add a single hour to your life?" – Matthew 6:27

Chapter One Coaching Question:

What are some of the greatest lessons you have learned from your failures, struggles, and tragedies in your life?

To read my leadership tribute Blog to Brittany Hibdon I wrote the week of her death, scan this QR Code and take note of the 3rd sentence in the blog, just under her picture.

Chapter 2

How Stubbornness Nearly Got Me Killed

You already know I'm a planner. It should come as no surprise then that I'm also regimented and can be more than a little stubborn, particularly when I think I know best. This can be another common failing of humans. We think we know better than our families, our spouse, our neighbors, our coworkers, our doctors. Some of us even think we know better than God what is true or good or right for us. God was about to show me how much I had to learn!

It was Friday, December 3rd, 2021, about 1:00 a.m., and I was just finishing work, doing my thing. All of a sudden, I felt this overwhelming cold. At first, I thought my furnace must have gone out, but the thermostat read 72 degrees. Before long, it was like an icy grip of death was surrounding my heart and my body. I was shivering uncontrollably. I went upstairs from my home office home, and I took my temperature. It was 104.8. I remember thinking, *It's a good thing this happened on a Friday. In a couple days I'll be feeling better, and I'll be able to get back to work.* I couldn't have been more wrong.

The next day, the fever was still the only symptom I had. I laid in bed, and I still had a very high fever that hit 105.1 by noon. I took more Tylenol which knocked it down to 102. I didn't believe I had COVID at first because I had heard COVID caused a low-grade fever with a cough and runny nose. Then Sunday rolled around and all three of my kids, Jack, Ava, and Emma, all start coughing and having stomach issues like cramps and diarrhea. Around the same time, I start coughing and having intermittent runny noses.

At this point my wife, Monica, thought we all had COVID, so she went and got a take-home COVID test, and all of us, except for her, had positive results. This is when my wife transformed into the Archangel Michael, and became this super-powered being, going to war to fight off COVID to protect her family. She became so powerful.

Over the next few days, I started feeling a heaviness in my chest, and Monica was taking care of me and the kids. Monica decided that it was time to go to the doctor. So, she took me to an Urgent Care clinic, and the doctor pulled out a stethoscope and put it to my chest. He was a young man, couldn't have been over 26, and when he started listening to my breathing, his face turned ghost white. He said, "You need x-rays and a CT scan now."

They put me in the x-ray machine, and then they got me CT scans. He came back to me and asked me how long I'd had COVID. I shared with him that it was since December 3rd, and he nervously said, "I hate to be the bearer of bad news, but you have severe COVID pneumonia. And based on how much fluid is in your lungs, you look like a patient that is two weeks to three weeks in because I've never seen someone on day six have that much COVID pneumonia. It's progressed very fast. I've never seen someone with that much fluid in their lungs so quickly. I'm

Chapter 2: How Stubbornness Nearly Got Me Killed

going to prescribe you a Zpack, codeine for your cough, and an albuterol inhaler to help open your airways. I would recommend getting a monoclonal antibody treatment. I'm going to put you in for one, but because you're on day 6 you're past our 5-day protocol for that."

My wife immediately sprung into action. She called around and found a doctor an hour and a half down south who was able to give me a monoclonal antibody infusion. There, they gave me IV fluids and looked at my oxygen levels. She said they were low and recommended to Monica that I get oxygen concentrator in my house to help keep my blood oxygen levels up. They referred Monica to another doctor who was able to get me ivermectin. Monica was able to get Hydroxychloroquine from another doctor. They gave me Tylenol to reduce my fever and more antibiotics to try to fight any bacterial infection in my lungs.

Early the next day, a technician showed up at my house with a hospital-grade oxygen concentrator. It was a machine that created 10 Liters of Oxygen. My wife was able to accomplish so much in the face of adversity. I couldn't believe how she did these things. I don't know how she was able to become so powerful while I just laid in bed, waiting for her care.

The doctors told me later that because of all the things Monica did to treat my COVID, that's a big factor in why I survived. My wife played a huge part in saving my life, but check this out. Even with all this medicine, the oxygen, the ivermectin, the hydroxychloroquine, I kept declining each and every day.

About four days later, I was lying in my bedroom, and even with the O2 concentrator, my oxygen started dipping into the

80s again one night. Monica called the doctor who advised her to get me more oxygen. At about 3:00 a.m., a technician showed up at my house with a second concentrator. They connected them together in some sort of daisy chain and upgraded my nasal oxygen tube with a mask and air bag. At that point, I was breathing in 20 liters of O2 from a reservoir oxygen mask. This stabilized my oxygen at 90 for a few more days, yet I kept declining. Each day, it was harder to breathe and keep my oxygen up. Each sleepless night, my once comfy mattress was like rolling around on a bed of knives. When I would stand up, my knees ached and my feet throbbed in pain.

December 15th, twelve days after coming down with symptoms, when I walked, I experienced massive pain in my feet and legs. What I didn't understand yet, and would learn from doctors in the hospital, was that one of the three ways COVID attacks is with inflammation of organs and joints. COVID was inflaming my muscles, joints, and organs, causing severe leg pain when I walked. Also, due to the organ swelling, I couldn't get comfortable in my bed. No matter how I would position myself, all I felt was stabbing pain throughout my body.

The night of December 17th, I needed to use the restroom, but I didn't feel like experiencing the pain in my legs and feet. On top of that, I was coughing so hard I couldn't stand up. Luckily, I had a Gatorade bottle next to me. I filled it up with urine, closed it, and went back to sleep. Peeing in a bottle was something I hadn't done since my deployment to Iraq in 2003 when I was a Special Operations Sergeant in the Army and spent days in the turret of a Humvee while driving through the desert.

Chapter 2: How Stubbornness Nearly Got Me Killed

The next morning, I had just woken up, and I had to use the restroom again. I attached the Oxy-Pulsometer to my finger, 89. I stood up, and as soon as I shifted my weight to my feet, it felt like I was standing on broken glass. My knees screamed in agony, and it felt like someone stabbed me in my lower back with a knife. I gasped for air, breathing very quickly, breaths coming more and more shallow as I reeled forward toward the bathroom. I watched the Oxy-Pulsometer in horror as my blood oxygen level quickly dropped down from 89 to the 50s. I was breathing in quick gasps of air, but like wrapping a plastic bag over your head and breathing in carbon dioxide, the air wasn't sating my lungs. I felt my heart pounding in my chest as it tried to compensate for the lack of oxygen before everything went dark.

I don't know if it was the pain in my legs and back or the lack of oxygen in my blood, but I had fainted. I woke up face down on the bathroom floor in front of the toilet in my own urine. I later found out from one of my nurses that the oxygen tube was pumping twenty liters of oxygen into my nose, and the prone position I had landed in probably kept me from dying right then and there.

Ironic how my first thought upon waking up was, "How can I clean up this mess so my poor wife, now sick with COVID, exhausted from caring for her family the last 3 weeks, doesn't have to clean it up?" I was able to accomplish that without standing up, thanks to some wet ones and a roll of toilet paper laying near where I had passed out.

"What if Monica had found me like that?" I asked myself. I was so glad I woke up before my wife found me there. She was so tired. The fight in her had gone, and now she needed to focus on her healing. She had been carrying the kids and me for the last three weeks, and now carrying me, while she was sick, was too great a burden.

My next thoughts turned toward the words Shawn Hibdon had used to describe Brittany Hibdon's passing in her home, "Her breaths were so shallow."

I thought of my breathing right before I fainted, realizing how my breaths kept getting more and more shallow even with all the oxygen that was being pumped into me. I realized that if I stayed at my house any longer, I would meet the same fate as Brittany. It was time to go to the hospital, at least there maybe I would have a fighting chance. Even with all that had happened with Brittany, and all that I was going through, I was still questioning my decision to go to the hospital.

I was terrified to go to the hospital. I will humbly admit, the seeds of fear, doubt, division, and distortion I allowed the media and online influencers to plant in my head had me on edge. Their assumptions, the opinions they spouted off as fact, and their fake causality of deaths tied to treatments had eroded my trust for the hospitals and medicine provided by doctors. Because of the evil propaganda that I took in, I feared experimental drugs that would destroy my kidneys. I had even heard hospitals were rewarded financially from COVID deaths. My plan had been to resist taking drugs and battle the doctors to keep the evil drugs out of my body!

Chapter 2: How Stubbornness Nearly Got Me Killed

Even though my wife had the same concerns with the hospitals and medicine, her words pointed me in the right direction, and the tears in her eyes told me to listen to her, "I've done everything I could, and you keep getting worse. I can't do anything else to help you, Sean. All night you cough and gasp for air, and I'm really scared. I'm sick and exhausted. Please let me call an ambulance for you."

Just before the paramedics strapped me to the wheeled stretcher, I hugged my wife and kids goodbye. I truly felt like my death sentence was being carried out. I kissed them each one last time and gave my wife instructions on what to do with our finances if I didn't make it.

LESSON LEARNED

<u>Be Proactive</u>

Never put off to tomorrow what you can do NOW! Prior to getting ill I put something off.

Chirp. Three minutes later... *Chirp.*

The day before I got COVID, the smoke detector in my basement started chirping.

I thought to myself, "I'll take care of that tomorrow."

That next day, the icy grip of the chills that came with that extremely high fever hit me, and I didn't get out of bed until the ambulance came to get me two and a half weeks later.

All day and night I heard *Chirp... Chirp... Chirp...* every three minutes, for weeks, it was maddening! One of the first things I heard when getting home from the hospital... *Chirp.* As soon as I was capable, my son and I took the smoke detector off the ceiling and smashed it with a rubber mallet.

Needless to say, the issue is now resolved, but this is a valuable lesson! Eliminate procrastination from your life! Because initiative is godly!

My wife Monica and I have been married for over 17 years. Growing up, she had always wanted a beautiful wedding in a Catholic Church. When I had just gotten out of the Army, I spent all my money buying my first house. And back then at the age of 23, faith was an afterthought. As a result, we ended up getting married in the St. Louis city courthouse. Then, in 2016, Monica lost the diamond in her engagement ring.

For years, I've been wanting to give her a real wedding in a Catholic Church and replace her lost diamond. But with business and life, I kept kicking the can down the road. Well, that was bullshit and excuses. And thanks to the severe COVID Pneumonia, I almost missed my chance forever. Thankfully, God gave me more time with my family! The lesson: *never* put off to tomorrow what you need to do *now!*

I decided to take care of this now, and it's brought even more love and faith into my family!

It's only too late to scratch something off your bucket list, make amends with a loved one, re-unite with an old friend, write a book, give to your church, donate to a nonprofit, spend time with family... once you die! Here's another thought. It's never too early to do those things either!

Chapter 2: How Stubbornness Nearly Got Me Killed

It's a good thing, in the words of my coach and dear friend Keith Rosen, "You don't only live once. You get to live every day."

Take advantage of that. Live right now!

- Don't wait to forgive someone you love
- Don't wait to spend time with your family
- Be healthy *now*
- Go to church and pray *now*
- When should you do what you know you should do? RIGHT NOW!

KEY SCRIPTURES

"I must work the works of Him that sent me, while it is day: the night cometh, when no man can work." – John 9:4

"The soul of the sluggard desireth, and hath nothing: but the soul of the diligent shall be made fat." – Proverbs 13:4

"He that observeth the wind shall not sow; and he that regardeth the clouds shall not reap." – Ecclesiastes 11:4

"For if any be a hearer of the word, and not a doer, he is like unto a man beholding his natural face in a glass: For he beholdeth himself, and goeth his way, and straightway forgetteth what manner of man he was. But whoso looketh into the perfect law of liberty, and continueth therein, he being not a forgetful hearer, but a doer of the work, this man shall be blessed in his deed." – James 1:23-25

Chapter Two Coaching Question:

What do you avoid and procrastinate that if you were on your death bed tomorrow and could no longer accomplish, would cause you the most regret?

To see the physical decline firsthand from Days 2, 6, and 15, respectively, scan the QR Code below:

Chapter 2: How Stubbornness Nearly Got Me Killed

In the first picture, I was still trying to convince myself I had the flu on day two. My daughter Emma had just given me water to "help Daddy feel better." When I asked her why the water tasted funny, she replied, I just gave the dog some water from the same cup.

Picture two was day six, and I had just arrived at urgent care. I was about to get the announcement that I had severe covid pneumonia.

My wife took pictures three on day fifteen. She had just called the ambulance and was waiting on their arrival. You can see my face bloated with death, as the swelling in my body was rampant due to covid.

Chapter 3

The Lowest Moment

In the ambulance, my paramedic was a large man with a thick but well-trimmed beard named Rich. He couldn't have been any more than thirty years old, but I could tell he was extremely skilled for his age. For such a big bearded guy, he had a very calming demeanor and very soothing presence. On the way there, he comforted me by saying the hospital was going to take great care of me. All the while he did everything he could to get my oxygen up, gave me a nebulizer treatment, and keep me awake and talking. He was kind and I could tell he cared, and when someone cares about you, you feel it.

The ambulance dropped me off at the emergency room entrance to the hospital and the paramedics quickly wheeled me into a room. A group of nurses moved me from the wheeled ambulance stretcher to the hospital bed, and there was a handful of ER nurses and doctors coming in and out of the room that began working to stabilize me. One immediately gave me an IV, another hooked my nose up to a device called a vapotherm that would pump 35+ liters of oxygen through the breathing tubes in my nose and into my lungs. When they put the tubes in my nose and turned it on, forcing live saving oxygen into my lungs it felt like I was sticking my head out of the window of a vehicle traveling down the highway at seventy miles per hour.

Another stripped me down and started gluing wires to my chest that would monitor my heart rate, breathing, and other vitals as long as I was in the hospital. Another nurse started getting my hospital gown ready to wear. They slipped their wired Oxi-Pulsometer onto my finger. The device that would measure my blood oxygen levels, which determined if the vapotherm was stabilizing my oxygen levels, or if things were getting worse.

As all this was happening, a doctor said, "As long as the vapo machine stabilizes your oxygen levels for long enough, we will move you to the severe COVID hospital floor called the 'Step down unit'. There, they will be able to keep you conscious and treat your COVID, and, as you begin to improve, lower the oxygen output to a more comfortable level. At some point, they'll get you off this device and onto something with lower oxygen output."

With what little strength I had, I nodded my head in understanding.

He cleared his throat and continued, "If your oxygen levels don't stabilize here, then we will need to put you on a ventilator, which would involve placing you in a medically induced coma. We would then move you to the ICU and continue your treatments there."

I was terrified of the prospect.

The doctors and nurses finished getting me set up in the ER and vacated the room. No more than an hour had gone by. I wasn't watching my own oxygen levels at the time, but the devices monitoring my vitals started to beep in an ominous way, alarms sounding.

Chapter 3: The Lowest Moment

All of a sudden, one of the ER nurses rushed into the room and looked over my stats, and doublechecked to see that everything was hooked up right. She made a call to the doctor who had consulted with me earlier. He came back into the room with a sense of urgency, along with most of his entourage. I could tell something was wrong, and I don't know if it was the fear, or the illness getting the best of me, but I felt extremely cold and kept shivering. Even with the vapo blowing oxygen into my lungs, each shallow breath felt like there was no oxygen for my body to consume. I don't know what dying feels like, but I remember thinking, it can't be much different than this.

While lying there completely helpless, without the energy to speak with the seven or so medical professionals that were in and out of my room, I heard them talking about the ventilators again. One nurse mentioned that my O2 levels still weren't stabilizing. I heard another mention something about a tracheotomy. The doctor began explaining to me that my lungs were failing, and to survive any longer I would need to be ventilated. One of the nurses began asking me if there was anyone else they should call and alert that I was going on the vent. I began to realize how bad off I was, and the feeling of fear intensified.

Just when I thought things couldn't get any worst, now I had to go number two. The last week had been a diet of soup, a wide variety of vitamins, a lot of fluids, and all those other medicines which had taken their toll on my digestive track. My stomach gurgled and I knew this was going to be diarrhea. I looked around the room and saw a toilet against one of the walls of the room. I tried to speak up to let the doctors and nurses know that

I needed to go to sit on that toilet now, but I couldn't muster the strength to get their attention. Even if I could have at the time, with all the wires and IV's I was connected to, I wouldn't have made it to the toilet. It all came out right then and there, all over my legs, my back, my gown, and my bed.

A family friend is an ER nurse, and in the past she had told me about what nurses call a "code brown". That's when people who are bad off, or close to death, lose control of their bowels. I never expected to be one of them. At least not today, not at forty years old. And for a moment, I didn't even feel like I was human. I was embarrassed and ashamed. In that moment, I believed it was the weakest moment of my life.

LESSON LEARNED

<u>Be Vulnerable</u>

In retrospect, I needed this humbling experience, which was designed to teach me that I wasn't willing to be vulnerable. To be vulnerable is to be human, and every human has times where they need help from other humans. God was teaching me to accept my humanity and accept this gift of compassion and service from other humans.

What I want you to learn in reading that section is that there are times in life when you are called to help other people. And there are times in life when you are called to accept help from other people. Do both with open arms. In this way, both you

Chapter 3: The Lowest Moment

and those who would serve you are capitalizing on an opportunity to earn God's favor and make it to heaven.

The nurses looked upon me warmly with care and compassion. They told me not to worry and that they were going to get me all cleaned up. "We see this all the time. You'll be clean in a jiffy," one nurse said.

As a society we have become extremely prideful. We wear this pride like a shell around us because we think it keeps us safe. Why do you wear this shell? Maybe you are worried about how you will be viewed by others because inside you have a low self-image. Perhaps you don't want to give someone ammunition to use against you, because you fear judgment. Maybe you don't want to bring someone else down, so you always want to smile on the outside, regardless of how you feel on the inside. Maybe there are a dozen other reasons, but what you need to know is that nothing will protect you more than vulnerability. Because there are no perfect people on the planet, when you try to be one, everyone around you knows you're being fake. When you become vulnerable, you are being authentic, real, and are a person in need. Thanks to our deep human instinct to help others in need, when you become vulnerable you will attract those who want to serve and protect you. You will repel those who don't want to help you in need, and those people aren't meant to be with you when you're happy and healthy.

When my wife cried and told me she was exhausted and could no longer care for me, she became vulnerable. She helped me realize what she was going through, and, as a result, helped me find my way to the doctors and nurses that would save my life. Get vulnerable. It might save your career, your marriage, your relationships, or even your life.

KEY SCRIPTURE

"For I was an hungered, and ye gave me meat: I was thirsty, and ye gave me drink: I was a stranger, and ye took me in: Naked, and ye clothed me: I was sick, and ye visited me: I was in prison, and ye came unto me. Then shall the righteous answer him, saying, Lord, when saw we thee an hungered, and fed thee? or thirsty, and gave thee drink? When saw we thee a stranger, and took thee in? or naked, and clothed thee? Or when saw we thee sick, or in prison, and came unto thee? And the King shall answer and say unto them, Verily I say unto you, In as much as ye have done it unto one of the least of these my brethren, ye have done it unto me." – Matthew 25:30-40

Chapter Three Coaching Question:

How could opening up to others about what you feel weakest about help you overcome those obstacles?

Chapter 3: The Lowest Moment

To see the pic of Sean just days after leaving the ER, Visit the QR Code below:

After I woke up in what they called the Covid six step-down unit, the swelling in my face had gone down. I had just received my phone and had the strength to take a picture. And though my body was in agonizing pain, I felt blessed to be alive, and God's love filled my soul with joy.

Chapter 4

Miracles

Even though getting cleaned up and the nurse's compassion made me feel better emotionally, they were still prepping me for the ventilator. It seemed some of the nurses coming into the room were bringing in equipment to do just that. I shivered more from the icy cold grip of COVID pneumonia and lack of oxygen in my blood.

All of a sudden, I felt a new warm presence next to my bed. I looked over my right shoulder and standing right next to my bedside was Brittany. She was not in her human form, but that of a faintly glowing golden spirit. I could see her outline, which was an illuminating bright yellow, and her face and body were wispy and gray. I blinked twice in astonishment, wondering if I was hallucinating and waiting for her to vanish, but she was still there. I glanced around the room at the doctors and nurses coming in and out to see if they had any awareness of the new presence in the room. A nurse walked through her like an airplane would fly through a small cloud, with no hesitation or acknowledgment of her presence.

Brittany's wispy hand slowly reached out toward my chest, and at the exact same time I could hear her voice inside my head. "You're going to be okay. You are going to make it." She said to me as clear as day, without moving her lips or making an actual audible sound. It was definitely Brittany.

Her hand reached into my heart and lungs and immediately a warmth spread over my body starting from where her hand entered my chest. All of the sudden, I could breathe again. It was like stepping outside after a long cold winter into a beautiful warm spring day. The oxygen pumping from the vapo into my lungs felt like it had value. My shivering immediately subsided. The stabbing pain from the bed of knives that had kept me from sleeping for a week completely vanished. I felt no fear about dying and was overcome with sleepiness at the same time. I just wanted to take a nap, so I smiled and dozed off.

When I awoke, the ER nurses were getting ready to move me. I had no clue if I slept for an hour, a day, or a week. Wondering if I was in the ICU waking up with a ventilator on, I slowly reached a hand up toward my face. There was no ventilator, just the large tube from the vapo, still blowing air up my nose like a giant hair dryer.

The ER doctor said, "I've never seen that before. It was kind of miraculous how you just caught oxygen out of nowhere. As if your lungs found a hole in all that fluid to breath. Your oxygen has stabilized for long enough, so we're sending you up to the 6th floor, which is the severe COVID unit I mentioned before. Good luck."

I felt strong enough to speak. I asked, "Doctor, do you have me on some sort of pain killer, or something that could cause feelings of euphoria or hallucinations?"

"No. Not that we've given you," he replied.

Chapter 4: Miracles

As they wheeled me into my new hospital room on the 6th floor, I had no clue that I was going to spend the next week there. I had no clue I would be battling my own perceptions, my limiting beliefs, and the disease. Shortly after getting settled into my new bed, receiving a debrief on how to order food and call a nurse, I dozed off again.

I seldom remember my dreams, and when I do remember them, it's only bits and pieces. But during this sleep, I had the most vivid dream of my life. My body was lying in the hospital room sleeping, and I was floating near the ceiling of my room, looking down on myself. Suddenly, the floating version of myself was whisked away up into the night sky. I could look upon the entire earth, and, at first, I thought I was standing on the moon. It didn't take me long to realize that I was embraced by an extremely large being, at least 20 times the size of our planet. I was being held in his massive right arm, though it was like standing on the great salt flats in Utah. I felt infinite love from the being that was embracing me. In that moment my perspective changed, I was soaring back toward earth. I looked back to see where I was standing, and it was a massive outstretched arm. I could see millions of tiny little yellow glowing spirits, surrounding the being. Like a magnet pulling a paper clip, my spirit was pulled back toward my body at great speed.

When I awoke, things were different. *I* was different. I was experiencing the most amazing paradox. My legs felt like they were battered and beaten with baseball bats. My lungs felt like there was gravel mixed with molten plastic in them, and my head felt like someone had beaten it with a tire iron. Even though my body was broken, my soul was filled with joy and hope. It felt like my heart was a 10-ounce glass, and it was somehow holding all the water from all the oceans. Except the oceans filling my heart weren't water but were faith and love. In my adult life, I could count on one hand the number of times I had cried. For the first time in my life, I was crying tears of joy.

The feelings were washing over me in waves, and they were so powerful. I felt God's loving embrace and the prayers from hundreds of families, friends, loved ones, and strangers. I could hear people praying for me. I could see people praying when I would close my eyes. I saw old friends praying for me whom I hadn't seen in years. Even strangers in other countries were praying for me.

I remember thinking, "This doesn't make sense. My wife and I didn't tell anyone except my employees and my coaching clients what was going on with my illness. How would all these people be praying for me without knowing I'm sick?"

Yet with every blink, I saw prayer. In every moment of silence, I heard prayer. With every waking moment, I felt prayers lifting me up.

The prayers were so overwhelmingly powerful, that even to write about and talk about them weeks later still almost brings me to tears.

Some prayers would wash through my body relaxing me and giving me peace, others were attacking the COVID virus-like artillery in combat. They were powerful and helped me get through the many battles I would face in the upcoming days.

Chapter 4: Miracles

It wasn't until two days later that I received my phone in a care package sent by my wife. Upon looking at my notifications I had hundreds upon hundreds of texts, messages on social media, videos from amazing people I coach, and voicemails from parishioners saying they were praying for me. Even my company's marketing team in India had posted a picture of me on a prayer board and asked for prayers.

I don't know if it was the healing touch of Brittany's spirit, the embrace by God in my dream, or the multitude of prayers that were enveloping my body and healing my soul or all three, but despite my body's decrepit condition, I felt absolutely amazing. I was happier than I had felt in years. Fears about my coaching clients leaving and my team not being able to hold the business together while I was sick were gone. Resentments toward my family members I used to hold onto, gone. Guilt about the lack of time I gave my family before, and the opportunities to do good I had missed in life, forgiven. It was as if I had a whole new baptism. I had a new, clean slate to conduct life, business, and faith, which would lead to great fulfillment and joy for myself, while helping me make a true impact on my brothers and sisters in Christ. This is what exactly what I needed to pull through. Thank you, God!

LESSONS LEARNED

<u>Be Watchful</u>

God's signs, wonders, and messages are all around us. Sometimes they are powerful and transformative. Other times, they are subtle but no less important. I've learned to proactively look for God everywhere.

Shortly after returning to work, I was sharing this story with a wonderful woman, a business controller I coach by the name of Sheryl. She had lost her son to a drug overdose not long ago. Her son had a wonderful spirit and piercing blue eyes. Soon after her son's passing, she noticed blue jays flying around and acting very strangely. Other people in her family even pointed out the thing, while asking Sheryl, "Do you think that's your son?" This gives her faith and hope while honoring her son, and showing God she believes.

<u>Be Faithful</u>

After briefly feeling God's unending love, I take great solace in the fact that my Dad, Jerry, my Grandparents, my military buddies and everyone else that has passed away gets to experience that for all eternity. Those you love are always watching over you, God is always watching over you, and God's love for you is infinite. The more you believe in God, and have faith that He is watching over you, while caring for all the loved ones that you have ever lost, the more you will receive His gifts.

You don't have to wait until you are on your death bed to accomplish this.

Months prior to this experience, a friend and coaching client became one of my mentors in faith. His name is Brian Dorsett, and we were discussing the power of faith. Brian is an ex-professional baseball player and one of the most devout Christians I know. He told me of a story where he and a good friend of his had one of the most powerful faith-based experiences of his life. In Brian's story, during a long and intense prayer session, Brian's heart filled with the Holy Spirit. It was so powerful that Brian felt God's love and strength so intensely that it exuded from his belly, and he began to speak in tongues. Upon hearing that story I thought, "Brian's so lucky to experience that." I never expected to have my own story where I would feel that way, yet here I was just months later being given my own experience.

KEY SCRIPTURES

"Be still, and know that I am God: I will be exalted among the heathen, I will be exalted in the earth." – Psalm 46:10

"And all things, whatsoever ye shall ask in prayer, believing, ye shall receive" – Matthew 21:22

"But without faith it is impossible to please him: for he that cometh to God must believe that he is, and that he is a rewarder of them that diligently seek him." – Hebrews 11:6

Chapter Four Coaching Question:

In your lifetime, who have you lost, that you know is watching over you and protecting you? Who is still part of your life, that is watching over you?

Chapter 5

Fear the Disease, Not the Cure

Being wheeled off in the ambulance was scary. The seeds of fear, doubt, division, distortion, and distraction I allowed the media to plant in my head had me scared, to say the least. I feared experimental drugs that would destroy my kidneys. I heard hospitals were rewarded financially from COVID deaths. When I said goodbye to my wife and kids that morning, I felt like my death sentence was being carried out. My plan was to resist and battle to keep the evil drugs out of my body! Here's how that fight went down.

The first doctor who came to me was a young woman, likely in her late twenties. She handed me a piece of paper with the title in bold at the top: "Fact Sheet for Patients, Parents and Caregivers Emergency Use Authorization (EUA) of Baricitinib".

My initial lizard brain response, trying to protect myself after all the seeds of doubt I allowed to be planted by social media and news, led me to react out of fear. "Oh great, I get to be a Guinea pig for experimental medicines," I thought.

The doctor explained that this was an anti-inflammatory that they give Rheumatoid Arthritis patients and that it has risks for blood clots. She said if that occurred, they would treat me for those with blood thinners. But this medicine was important because it would treat the immediate organ swelling and inflammation issue that I was having.

"I'm skeptical. This is what I was afraid of. When do you need an answer by?" I asked the doctor.

She looked frustrated and retorted, "Just don't call me at midnight when you can't breathe for this."

I didn't understand her reaction at the time, but I would find out a few minutes later where she was coming from when the Charge Nurse came into my room. She was a young mother and wife named Devann. She walked in wearing some hip green glasses that matched her medical gown, and her brown hair was styled perfectly. I could tell by the way she confidently navigated around my room checking the stats on my equipment that her skills were on point.

Based on her passion for her nursing career, it made me curious about her "why".

"Devann, why do you do what you do?" I asked her.

Her eyes lit up at the opportunity to share her purpose and she replied, "About ten years ago, I was in a severe car accident. It put me into the ICU. I spent 5 weeks in the hospital recovering. I had to learn to walk again."

She paused as tears welled up in her eyes, "The doctors and nurses took such great care of me, that it made me realize that this was my calling. If I can help other people recover in the same way, it's my way of paying it forward."

Her authenticity and genuine attitude toward selfless service built my trust with her immediately. I asked her, "Should I take this experimental Baricitinib drug?"

"Legally, I can't tell you what you should or shouldn't do. But what I can tell you is that our doctors are wise and talented. We have tested your blood. We've been working with COVID patients for two years now. We know how to save lives, the problem is..." she paused and got emotional.

"The problem is that there are people on their death bed, literally about to die of COVID, and they still don't believe COVID even exists. Patients like you come in here every day, fearful of us and the hospitals. They think the medicine is all experimental and it's going to kill them. They turn down the medicine and then..." She teared up.

"It's okay, take your time," I comforted her.

She composed herself and continued, "And then they wait until the 11th hour to say yes to the medicine... and by then it's too late. By then COVID has destroyed their organs, shredded their lungs, and clotted their blood. And then it's ventilator time, if they're lucky."

She put her hand on my arm and began searching for a vein to insert another IV into, "Look, Sean, you can trust us. We care about you, and we will do whatever it takes to save your life."

Just then the door swung open, and a completely masked man standing about 5 foot 10 walked in with poise. His name was Doctor B; that is, he goes by Doctor B.

When I met Dr. B, he was the ultimate professional. He took time to explain each medication they wanted to give me, how it worked, and why they used it. He promised to monitor me closely for safety. This included constant X-rays for clots or pneumonia and blood tests to make sure my kidneys were not over inflamed. He had me on a host of medications, including: steroids to remove the swollen tissue in my lungs, antibiotics to fight bacterial pneumonia infection, blood thinners to prevent clots since I couldn't walk, remdesivir to attack the virus directly, Baricitinib that they give rheumatoid arthritis patients to lower swelling in their organs, and others.

Throughout my entire stay, he constantly followed up, went over ALL my test results, and kept me informed as to exactly what was going on in my body and how everything was performing.

Even more important than what I thought of him, was what Dr. B's team thought of him. They called him at 3 a.m., and he ALWAYS answered and ALWAYS thanked them for calling. He always listened to them. He trusted his team and empowered them to solve problems. He was always guiding them as a coach. His team thinks he is genuine, humble, and authentic. He's one of them. He tells people what they need to hear, even if it hurts, because he believes truth is what matters, and he says TRUTH is care.

LESSON LEARNED

Be Educated

If you get sick, get to the doctor FAST. Trust these amazing humans with your heart, and they WILL treat it with care. Find a doctor who is transparent and honest about the medicines, and ensure they have a protocol for monitoring you throughout the medicinal utilization process. They WILL provide; the Lord WILL provide! You are NEVER alone!

There are professionals who are willing to help you who can cut through the fear, the misinformation, and the propaganda to help you make educated decisions about everything in your life, not just healthcare. Don't trust soundbites and social media hysteria. Get the facts and get help. When doubting someone's intent, ask them questions like, "What is so rewarding for you about this career?" and "WHY do you choose to do this?" You might just find out that you are dealing with some true professionals who really do care about you. Moreover, pray on the decisions you are making because God is with you. God loves you more than you can ever imagine!

God loves me so much that he put Monica in my life. My wife did a great job of educating herself at the beginning of my COVID experience. In fact, after I arrived at the hospital, the doctors told me that the decisive action Monica took to get me medicines saved my life. I proclaim that this woman is a true hero with God-like powers. I want you to know, that you have these latent abilities, too! God proclaims that marriage is a holy sacrament, and this is why. The Holy bonds of matrimony give your family power! Nothing can conquer you through Christ our Lord.

KEY SCRIPTURE

"Then you will know the truth, and the truth will set you free." – John 8:32

Chapter Five Coaching Question:

What areas of your life do you allow fear and assumptions to rule over education and confidence?

To check out a pic of hanging with Doctor B. after a weigh in when I had lost 38 pounds Scan the QR Code below:

My clothes were hanging off my body after losing 38 pounds. In this photo, I was able to stand up on my own for the first time in days. Doctor B had just gone through my XRays and blood work and let me know things were moving in the right direction. I am forever grateful for his honesty, care, and the way he leads his entire nursing team.

Chapter 6

The Power of Prayer and Love

After two days in my hospital bed, I opened the first care package from my wife. Two of the articles in the bag were my cell phone and charger. I decided to power the phone on and see what sort of notifications I had. Little did I know the blessing that awaited me in the form of several hundred text messages and several dozen videos.

It was my family, friends, and coaching clients. Many were pouring out thoughts and prayers which meant everything to me. There was another type of message I was receiving as well; this type of message was speaking to the core values I hold dear within my soul. I call these "legacy messages". Dozens of people I have been blessed enough to coach over the years had reached out to me, sharing how I had made a positive impact on their lives. It felt amazing to see the legacy I had been leaving, and it made me want to do even more.

In the Army, when setting up a base of operations, I was taught to always be improving your fighting position. In this way you become stronger, more entrenched, as time goes on and are best prepared for an enemy attack. The next unit to relieve you and take over the post is now set up for success. As a business consultant and executive coach, we call it continuous never-ending improvement. This is a process that ensures you don't backslide when the market changes around you, because you are continuously adapting to your surroundings. In this way you are proactive instead of reactive and constantly making things better. In life, I would simply call this the principle of leaving things better off than you found them. This way, no matter when you check out, you have left things better for the next generation. I believe we can leave a legacy by passing on knowledge, helping others achieve what they want in life, helping people grow in faith, and becoming better people overall.

Often, we go through life unaware of the legacy we are creating. We are just going to school, working each day, doing our jobs, going to stores, dealing with our family, hanging out with friends and so forth. In reality, every interaction is an opportunity to improve our position, and make an impact, by helping someone else improve. Because we as humans are part of the body of Christ, if one part of the body gets healthy, the entire body gets stronger. And sometimes it takes a near death experience for us to learn about our legacy. Most of the time, we don't get to find out about our legacy, but it's there regardless. One of my mentors, Chad Carden, always talks about how a butterfly flapping its wings on one side of the earth can start a hurricane on another side. I was able to see a beautiful example of this throughout my experience.

Throughout my hospital stay, I asked almost every nurse, "What made you want to be a nurse?"

When I asked Abby, an extremely positive and energetic evening shift respiratory therapist, this question, she had a beautiful story.

Chapter 6: The Power of Prayer and Love

She talked about how rough the birth of her son was. She almost died, along with her baby boy. Abby told me, "The nurses pulled out all the stops to make sure my son and I would pull through. It made me want to do the same thing for other people."

"And now that you're on the job, what do you love most about it?" I asked.

She values her career path so much, she had an answer right away, "I'm so glad I chose to nurse. It's the most rewarding job on the planet! The other day there was a woman who was covered in EKG glue from the sticky pads we use to attach the wires to them. They were all in her hair, and she felt gross because of it. She was too weak to wash it out herself. I helped her shampoo the gunk out of her hair, and afterwards she felt good. It makes me feel good to help other people feel better, and it's only right that I pay it forward after all the nurses did for me during my rough childbirth."

Fast forward to February 10th, 2022. My 6-year-old daughter Emma stops me as I am working on editing this very book. "Daddy, it's hero day at school tomorrow and guess what I am going to be?"

I smiled, rubbing my eyes after a two-hour writing session. Happy for the break, I asked, "What hero are you going to be?"

"You have to guess, Daddy!" she mischievously grinned.

"Wonder Woman?" I guessed.

"No, I'm going to be a doctor!" she replied confidently.

That decision filled my heart with joy, and I asked, "Why did you choose to be a doctor for hero day?"

"Because they saved you, Daddy. They are heroes." She wrapped her tiny arms around me and gave me the most amazing hug.

Do you see what's going on here? Do you see how the legacy flows forward and continues to impact people down the line? Do you see the power that we have? Abby's nurses doing good for her inspired Abby to go into the medical field. Abby and the nurses and doctors did good for me, and they inspired my daughter to be a doctor. I only hope Emma is smart enough to get scholarships to pay for medical school when the time comes so I don't have to foot the bill. Just kidding! I digress. Do you see the power we hold? But it makes sense! Why wouldn't you, a child of God and sister or brother to Jesus Christ, be able to influence someone's life so profoundly, by doing acts of good?

Abby's nurses probably didn't wake up the day of Abby's son's tragic birthday thinking, "I am going to impact someone's life and create a legacy of my own!"

It's more likely that they rolled out of bed, got dressed, went to work, and started doing what they do best—delivering babies and saving lives when the need arose.

That being said, when you do good, you inspire and affect others around you to do good. Really, it doesn't matter what your profession is; all that matters is who you are. Because who you are affects how you treat people. You might be surprised if you could see how far your reach goes and the legacy you are leaving behind.

Your life is a gift from God, and every chance you get to interact with someone is a chance to make a positive impact. We can never miss a chance to make a positive impact. At the end of your life, the interactions with the people you have touched are your legacy. The knowledge and inspiration you have given to others are your legacy. Be intentional about doing God's work. Be deliberate about bringing people joy. Be focused about sharing scripture and knowledge that will make others better. It's a great way to bring His Kingdom to earth. I believe one day when you stand before God, if you have left the right legacy behind, you will be rewarded. And nothing is more rewarding than experiencing God's unending love for all eternity.

LESSON LEARNED

<u>Be Grateful</u>

Getting messages from so many who were praying for me and who cared about me was overwhelming. I experienced a deep sense of gratefulness, love, and connectedness with all of them. Seeing the world through grateful eyes changes your perspective. I understood now what I meant to others and how I helped them. Too often, we don't let those we love and care for know how much they are appreciated; how grateful we are for them until it is too late.

On the morning of December 3rd, if you'd told me I would soon be taking a shower in a chair with an oxygen tank, I would have laughed at you. That morning, I remember forgetting my

"Nespresso" upstairs and running up to go grab it with ease. Today, I can't safely climb a flight of stairs alone, but I'm working on it!

My nurse Ben in the hospital said, when you get COVID you can lose all the "small stuff". I want to talk about "the small stuff" and the two things you should do with "the small stuff".

Appreciate the Small Stuff

Today as you do the following things smile! Fill your heart with gratitude and appreciation that you have the health and strength to do them. Enjoy it! Each of these small things is a thing of beauty!

Love tying your shoes!
Rejoice in walking upstairs!
Celebrate picking up one of your kids!
Find joy in getting yourself a glass of ice water!
Appreciate taking three breaths without pain!

Did you know, you can't feel hate, anger, or frustration along with appreciation at the same time? If you want to feel genuinely happy and fulfilled, start practicing appreciation while you have the ability to do the little things.

"For where your treasure is, there will your heart be also." – Matthew 6:21

Chapter 6: The Power of Prayer and Love

Don't Sweat the Small Stuff

Bringing up my dear friend and client Sheryl Orlen again, who lost her beautiful son, Aaron. She told me that one thing this trauma taught her was, "Don't sweat the small things." Because once horrible tragedy strikes on a grand scale none of that "small stuff" matters anymore.

In life, you get what you focus on. If you focus on all the "bad things" that are "happening to you," you are victimizing yourself. In victimizing yourself, you eliminate all chance for getting what you really do want. This is because everything is made first in our minds, and then in reality. Not the other way around. Imagine the life you do want, focus on that, and it comes to reality! Focus on what you don't want, and it keeps happening.

Can you imagine how hard it would be for your local sandwich delivery shop to get your order right if you called them and told them what you *don't* want?

"Jimmy John's may I take your order?"
"Yeah, I don't want a pizza..."

So today practice letting go of little stuff. Let go of any resentment toward one of your family members. Forgive a co-worker's transgression. Don't cry over spilled milk. Wave, smile, and truly love someone who cuts you off in traffic. When one of your kids isn't "perfect," let them be themselves. Instead, let go of those little frustrations and visualize what you do want to happen and move towards making that a reality.

Life is SO good, and God IS Everything! Today, cherish all that you are, all that you have, and truly fill your own soul with gratitude.

KEY SCRIPTURES

"One generation shall praise thy works to another, and shall declare thy mighty acts." - Psalms 145:4

"Let all bitterness, and wrath, and anger, and clamour, and evil speaking, be put away from you, with all malice: And be ye kind one to another, tenderhearted, forgiving one another, even as God for Christ's sake hath forgiven you." – Ephesians 4:31-32

Chapter Six Coaching Questions:

What would it mean for you, if all the things you love most about your life only existed because of the struggles and pain you have been through?

What are some of the small things you will internalize more appreciation for? And on the contrary, what are some of the small problems you can let go of frustration about?

To check out a video of Abby and I talking about the impact of delivering Cards for Covid patients visit the QR Code below:

Abby was one of my respiratory therapists; she wants to grow as a leader within the hospital. I felt both blessed and honored to have been able to give her some coaching to help her develop her confidence and communication. Throughout my stay in the hospital, I met many heroes. I felt the pain of their loss when patients wouldn't make it out of the step-down unit. But, on the other hand, I also felt the joy when they could heal someone and get them out of the hospital. Abby embraced the *cards for covid* immediately and started using them to impact her patience right away positively. When the chips are down, it's essential to use every tool available to heal physically and emotionally. She helped me do both, and then we worked together to do the same for others!

Chapter 7

It is Always Darkest Just Before the Dawn

The third night in the hospital was perhaps my darkest.

Ben was one of the nurses who had been caring for me throughout each evening at the hospital. Ben is in his mid-20s, is one of the most brilliant people I've ever met, and has one of the biggest hearts I've ever felt. The moment he walked into my room, he had a huge smile that I could hear through his mask and a ton of positive energy. He locked eyes with me, and the first words out of his mouth were, "Hi, I'm Ben, and we are going to get you through this."

Ben told me that he believes people deserve to be healthy, and his greatest joy about his job is seeing people will themselves to heal. He says, "Life is all about enjoying the small moments, being self-sufficient, and people who come in here have lost those things. They don't get to hear their baby cry, they can't go to the bathroom on their own, they can't turn on their own lights... It's my job to get them those things back!"

He feels so rewarded to be part of that COVID team because of how much they care, and how great his team is. He says that without the support of his coworkers, he would have failed long ago. His team helps him cope with the trauma they see when they lose patients. Sometimes, Ben works so hard that he doesn't want to let his team or his patients down, so he holds off going to the bathroom for an entire fourteen-hour shift.

His biggest fear is how losing patients is affecting his mental health long-term. He told me that every time he loses a patient, it breaks his heart because he loves each of us so much. He let me give him some coaching on this, and he realized that to continue to help people long-term, he has to stay centered and healthy within himself first. I asked him if this battle with COVID was a sprint or a marathon, and he said a marathon.

I asked him how he needed to run the race differently, and he said, "Sean, you have shown me that it's okay to be vulnerable, that I can share how I truly feel, and that people won't judge me. That alone is going to change my life and help me sustain this because I am going to start telling others how I feel." We hugged it out.

That night, Ben was the nurse watching over me, protecting me. He noticed I was breathing oddly at about 1 a.m. Ben listened to my chest and noticed there was not enough sound coming from the lower portions of my lungs. He had them set me up with a CT scan in the middle of the night. We found out I have PE (pulmonary embolisms) otherwise known as blood clots in my lungs. As a result, Ben got me extra blood thinners in the form of IV fluids, and shots in my stomach, which was likely a life-saving action.

Ben was my personal hero, and another guardian angel in the hospital. Throughout my discussions, I realized almost every nurse and doctor struggling on the front lines are dealing with the same thing Ben is. They each have their own stories of epic saves and heart-wrenching losses. I spoke with a number of them, and with the strength God and your prayers gave me, I did what I could to help those who were helping me. I did this by giving them the best coaching I could with the time we had together. One of the nurses started calling my hospital room "The coaching office". I felt so blessed to be a part of their lives.

Doctors and Nurses of the COVID, Cancer, ICU's, Step Down Units or other serious illness units. I had no clue before, but after living in your world for a couple of weeks, and spending countless hours learning about your goals and challenges, I now know what you are going through.

I know many of you can't count on your hands and toes how many times you had to hold a patient's hand while they took their last breath. You perform this task bravely.

I understand that many of you remember all the names or faces of the patients that don't make it. You carry this burden willingly.

You struggle with patients who don't trust the health care system, won't take the life-saving medicines, or don't believe COVID even exists right up to the point that they are about to go on a ventilator or die. You feel helpless to save these people.

You battle with patients and their family members when a 95-year-old patient doesn't have the will or desire to fight COVID and wants to go to their Lord in heaven, but the family members at home are demanding you save them. Being put in situations like that probably isn't what you signed up for as a nurse. You try so hard to make everyone happy.

You are worried about taking care of your patients. You want to help as many as possible but due to the full hospitals and limited equipment you find yourself having to make difficult choices about who gets treatment and who doesn't. You must follow protocol that doesn't have empathy or understanding.

Sometimes, you feel like you have no one to talk to and that discussing your feelings isn't good to do because A. you don't want to put a burden on others, and B. you don't know if it's okay to feel the way you do inside.

Due to extremely low staffing, when nurses in other departments quit, and they pull your team members from your unit, you have to do more with less. Also, losing a teammate is a struggle because sometimes they are your closest friends and greatest allies in this fight.

I know the traveling nurse companies are constantly recruiting you, trying to offer you more money to zip around to different hospitals, and you're constantly having to choose between your team and stability or more money for your family.

I know how much you thrive when you get to wheel a patient you helped recover out of the hospital, and you see them reunited with their family members and loved ones. But it doesn't happen enough for you.

As a result of the assault hell is making on heaven, with us as humans caught in-between, we are going through some of the darkest times in modern history. And this is exciting!

Okay, now I know you had to do a double take on that last sentence. No, I am not celebrating the dark times, what I am saying is simply this. For every dark night there is a bright day, and it's always darkest just before the dawn. You are making a difference each day, you are saving lives, keeping families together, and inspiring many to get involved in medicine with your love and care for your patients. Thanks to your love, dedication, and heroism, you are seeing us through these dark times. You are learning more about how to keep people alive each day and sharing that knowledge with your patients and medical communities. Advances in medicine are making an impact, and more people are turning to God again realizing that faith is salvation. My vow to you is that the truth, God's truth, about what you do, who you are, and why you do it will shine like one thousand suns. And Satan's darkness can't hide this powerful truth forever.

Things are going to turn around and soon because God is with you, I stand with you, everyone who gets to hear my story, and the truth will stand with you. The sun is going to come up soon, and you will bask in God's glory. The pain and suffering you're experiencing in this life can be a sacrifice to help you earn eternal life. Rest easy, that "this too shall pass".

LESSON LEARNED

Be Vigilant

Ben watching over me, listening to my breathing in the middle of the night, then taking action saved me. If he hadn't been watchful, vigilant, I might not be alive to be writing this. I owe him, and all the other doctors and nurses who kept watch over me, everything.

Too often in our lives we get busy, distracted, and lose focus. We forget to pay attention to what really matters. This experience reminded me that we need to pay attention to the work we've been called to do and to be on the lookout for the wiles of the enemy.

During my deployment to Iraq, the first time an IED (improvised explosive device) or roadside bomb exploded in our convoy was eight months into the war. It didn't happen during the first half of our deployment because then we were all hyper vigilant, watching closely for anything that could cause us harm. After six months of driving the same route we had always driven, we became complacent. We stopped paying close attention to our route, and no one noticed the pile of rocks on the side of the road with wires sticking out. As soon as our convoy got close, BOOM! In the Army we have a saying, "Stay alert, stay alive."

Sometimes in business and in life, we feel something is amiss because we're not getting the results we want, yet we don't pay close enough attention or seek to understand what's causing the bad result. If we don't understand what's causing a negative outcome, we can do nothing about it. I was coaching with the CEO of a multi-million dollar SAAS company, software as a service, here in St. Louis. After a couple of their clients cancelled, he was stressed out. What bothered him more than losing the clients was the fact that he was having trouble figuring out WHY they cancelled. He didn't know what to do to solve the issue, because he couldn't identify what was wrong. After an hour of coaching together, and about 30 coaching questions, he realized what was going on. Through my coaching questions, he found that his focus needed to be on serving their users instead of schmoozing the higher up check writers. As a result of this conversation, he fundamentally changed the way his company supported the front-line users among his clients. This led to client retention, and long-term growth. The CEO's vigilance in seeking out coaching on what could have been simply dismissed as "normal churn" led to great success.

KEY SCRIPTURE

"Be sober, be vigilant; because your adversary the devil, as a roaring lion, walketh about, seeking whom he may devour:" - I Peter 5:8

Chapter Seven Coaching Questions:

Where do you find yourself complacent as it relates to your own well-being, and the well-being of those you love? How can you be more vigilant in those areas?

To watch the video where Ben and Abby wheel me out of my room for the first time in days for a late night CT scan, and see my midnight reaction to the blood clots they found in my lungs, scan the QR Code here:

When battling severe illness, there are extreme peaks and valleys. These two videos give you the stark contrast in emotion that one goes through. One moment, you're experiencing a win, and you're on top of the world. The next moment, you're smacked in the face with bad news and realize how close to the edge you are.

I was so excited to leave my hospital room for the first time in days in video one. I celebrated that with Ben and Abby!

That night, I got the news I had developed blood clots in my lungs, and they were hooking me up to heavy doses of blood thinners to try and prevent the pulmonary embolisms from suddenly claiming my life.

Chapter 7: It is Always Darkest Just Before the Dawn

Psalm 23:4 gave me comfort that night.

The Lord *The Shepherd of His People*

A Psalm of David.

The Lord *is* <u>a</u>my shepherd; I shall not <u>1</u>want.
He makes me to lie down in green pastures;
He leads me beside the still waters.
He restores my soul;
He leads me in the paths of righteousness
For His name's sake.
Yea, though I walk through the valley of the shadow of death, I
    will fear no evil;
For You *are* with me;
Your rod and Your staff, they comfort me.
You prepare a table before me in the presence of my enemies;
You anoint my head with oil;
My cup runs over.
Surely goodness and mercy shall follow me
All the days of my life;
And I will dwell in the house of the Lord
Forever.

Chapter 8

God's Plan

If you haven't figured it out by now, I have always been a work hard, play hard kind of guy. Thus, my routine for the last few years has been to grind 10 hours a day, and then take a week off every quarter. The December I came down with covid, I had a week vacation planned between Christmas and New Year's. This is one of the reasons why I worked so hard that last week of November and first few days of December. My plan was to get ahead of work, that way I could unplug and enjoy time off without stress. Also, we had a family Christmas party scheduled at our home, it was going to be a great family get together.

When I got sick Friday December 3rd, one of my first thoughts was, "It's a good thing I got sick Friday night. I'll be able to go right back to work first thing Monday morning!"

Then Monday morning, December 6th rolled around, and I was still dreadfully sick with a 104 fever, and confirmed I had COVID. By Tuesday morning, I changed my plans. I thought, "Okay, I'll just make this week my vacation week, and I will work the week I was planning on taking off. At least my covid will be gone so we can still have the family Christmas party."

December 18th on my ambulance ride to the ER, I was still making plans. I continued to grip the steering wheel of my life, trying to impose my will and control everything. As the ambulance rushed toward the hospital I remember thinking, "We've got the Christmas party coming up later this week. I need to be home in a couple days to prepare for it."

After my near-death experience in the emergency room, many nights struggling to breathe, the realization that the death happening around me on the floor I was staying on could easily include me at any moment, the opportunity to give coaching and emotional support to the amazing nurses serving me, and a few serious conversations with my doctors I came to a powerful realization.

I was blessed to be alive.

God had put me there for a reason. He sent Brittany's spirit to bring me back for a reason. I was still alive and still at the hospital because God wanted me there. This realization helped me tremendously, and, for the first time in my life, I let go of my agenda. I trusted God's plan with all of my heart, and it felt so liberating. Here was the evidence of my change.

December 22nd one of my amazing doctors drew a picture on the "Goals" section of the whiteboard on my wall. It was a house with a Christmas tree in it.

The doctor said, "Let's see if we can get you home to your family for Christmas."

I smiled at him and said, "God willing." I had no agenda to make it home if God wanted me at the hospital.

Text messages started rolling in from friends and family members asking, "Are you going to make it home for Christmas?"

My reply was always the same, "I am right where God wants, and I will be where He wants me, when He wants me there, and wherever that is, I am happy!" And inside I truly felt content.

It didn't matter if I was home with my beautiful wife and kids or sitting at the hospital with the amazing doctors and nurses on Christmas. What mattered is that I had given God control, and that I was alive. I slept like a log that night, at peace.

The morning of December 23rd, one of the respiratory therapists came into my room. He had a special battery powered blood oxygen and pulse measuring device in one hand and a mobile oxygen tank on wheels in tow in the other. "Good morning, Sean, it's time for your walking test. If you pass this, and the doctors like what they see from your last blood draw, there's a good chance you'll get home by Christmas."

I smiled and thanked God, but my gratitude was not because I was going to be tested and would potentially be home for Christmas. I thanked God because He knew I had learned my lesson, and He was rewarding me. He would allow me to be with my family on the birthday of Jesus. From now on, it would always be God's will and not my own.

LESSON LEARNED

Be Willing to Let Go

We make plans, and we hold onto them with all our humanly strength. We become annoyed, or angry when things don't go our way. When you give up control to God, the paradox is that you become empowered. This is because you no longer have an agenda that you are clinging to, and this creates freedom. Freedom to find value and peace exactly where you are, no matter the circumstances.

I reflected on other times in my life when I refused to give control over to God, or just didn't know how. One of note was the last few months I was in Iraq. I became fearful and depressed, and this negatively affected my performance as a team member and combat leader. I was fearful that I would never make it home, and depressed because the deployment was taking far longer than expected. I just wanted to be with my girlfriend Monica and spend the money I saved up while on deployment. If I had the power to let go, and faith that God's plan was at work then, I could have been a better team member, and ultimately made a bigger positive impact before I left the country. While I don't regret anything, I do understand how this mindset would have made some of the most challenging, stressful, and roughest times in life, joyful.

When I got out of the hospital, I found out one of my clients had concerns with some of the project work that had gone on in my absence. The old fear of loss started to well up inside. Instead, I remembered what I had learned, and I gave control over to God. "God, if part of your plan is to continue working with this client, let it be so. If it isn't, I know you will provide!" As a result, I had one of the most productive conversations with them ever. We adapted to the situation, and we will continue to work together.

When you humbly ask for God's will to be fulfilled in you, while you truly give up your plan to Him, you will feel more confidence in your approach. You will perform better in most situations knowing that regardless of the outcome, God has a plan for you.

KEY SCRIPTURES

"Saying, Father, if thou be willing, remove this cup from me: nevertheless, not my will, but thine, be done." – Luke 22:42 (KJV)

"'For I know the plans I have for you,' declares the Lord, 'plans to prosper you and not to harm you, plans to give you hope and a future.'" – Jeremiah 29:11 (NIV)

Chapter Eight Coaching Question:

Where in your life do you need to let go of your agenda, and put your trust into a higher power?

Check out the picture of the "Goals" board with the house (just before the doctor added a Christmas tree) by Scanning the QR Code Below:

Health care providers use boards like this to keep the patient up to date with who's caring for them. At this point, they wanted me to get my activity level up, which was depicted in the up arrow, and for me to make it home, hence the picture of a house. On top of that, one of the nurses and I were discussing good shows to watch, and she recommended I watch "Alien Worlds". Also, the soap I was using to wipe down my body each day was causing me to break out in a rash. So, they told me not to use that soap anymore. On the board, you can see "No CHG Soap". The info on the board was invaluable and amusing notes would lift my spirits.

Chapter 9

Here Comes the Sun

I will never forget what happened as Devann hooked up my oxygen tank and wheeled me out to see my wife who was waiting out front of the hospital so she could drive me home on Christmas Eve. She called in a COVID recovery to someone in the hospital, and throughout the entire building, the song "Here Comes the Sun" by the Beatles played on the intercom. Devann told my wife how awesome of a patient I was, and she gave me one of the best hugs I've ever gotten in my life. I could tell she was filled with joy to see that she had saved another life and helped one of her patients recover, just like she experienced as a patient 10 years ago after her accident. I cried with tears of gratitude and joy as I held my wife, and I couldn't thank enough Devann, the other nurses, the doctors, the respiratory therapists, the nurse's assistants, the nutrition staff, and everyone else who gives so much to save lives.

Upon arriving at home, it was the most beautiful reunion. The dog was barking, my kids were screaming, and we were all crying tears of joy. I could barely breathe walking into my house, even with my oxygen tank full blast, but the reunion was well worth all the struggle.

My kids and I spent hours talking about the last couple of weeks. They wanted to know every detail about the hospital. At the same time, we sat beside the Christmas tree and fireplace talking about how Santa probably wasn't going to bring us much this year. After all, why would Santa want to set foot into a COVID-infested house? In reality, my wife and I had completely missed an entire month of Christmas shopping due to COVID. It didn't matter. We didn't need presents because being alive and together was all that mattered.

Since my return home, my kids and I have listened to the song "Here Comes the Sun" about two dozen times. My wife is sick of it, but that's okay. Because God is light, He created it on the first day of Genesis. Most diseases such as COVID and cancer thrive in darkness and feed off fear and anxiety, but God is with us, and the dawn is coming. Please take a moment to pray and thank God for making these amazing health care professionals, and ask that He continue to give them strength, health, and peace of mind so that they may continue to fight this fight until that beautiful sun breaks the horizon.

LESSON LEARNED

Be Joyful

People ask me all the time, "How do you stay so positive?" and "Have you ever said anything negative?" because there is so much to be happy about, and not much to be negative about. I have found in life that lifting up the spirits of others is the ultimate path to joy. Most people are going through so much in their lives that if someone would just make them smile, it can change their entire world for the better. If "lifting other's spirits" and "being joyful" is what we want to accomplish, how do we make that happen? The path begins inside you, by changing your filter. To create joy, the filter you must sift everything through is love and gratitude. Even though this isn't easy to do, when you understand how, you will learn you have total control over this.

First, understand how our minds work regarding experiences translated into attitude. Every environmental stimulus you encounter is first filtered through your senses: hearing, sight, touch, taste, and smell. Next, your brain takes that input and decides in milliseconds: good OR bad. A bad reaction will equal a negative output. The greatest challenge is that our brains are always trying to protect us by looking for the danger in our environment, and as such bad triggers are more common than good.

Don't believe me or need more clarity? Ever had one of those mornings where "nothing went right"? You spilled your coffee, argued with your spouse, got cut off in traffic, and had unruly customers at work? If you're like most, you were probably all kinds of salty and frustrated! Thoughts like, "Dammit, today's going to suck" and "My spouse is a BEEP" and "This jerk doesn't know how to drive" and "I'm sick of these BLEEPING customers," probably crossed your mind. Am I accurate here?

You likely didn't realize how blessed you are to have these problems, and didn't probably think about it like this:

- Good, less caffeine means I will be less anxious today.
- We're still married after all these years!
- I made it safely to work without an accident!
- I'm so glad I have a paying job where I get to help customers!

And therein lies your opportunity to change your lens to that of love. Everything has an upside. It's the journey of life that matters, not where you end up. When you love the things you shouldn't, you are changing your attitude about things. As a result, your reactions become authentically positive, and coming from a place of love you can't help but lift others up. And as you lift others up, you are filled with joy.

I was coaching a frustrated sales manager around this exact challenge. He shared how one of his veteran sales consultants still brings incomplete paperwork for his sales.

I asked, "How does this make you feel?"

And he replied, "Angry and frustrated."

And I asked, "Then how do you react?"

He replied, "I hold it in, because I used to get in trouble for yelling at people."

I asked him to change his lens, "If you were coming from a place of love for your employee and gratitude, how would you feel instead?"

After some thought he replied, "I'm grateful I get to be a manager because this employee isn't perfect, and I would want to help them get better instead of want to yell at them."

"Beautiful, and how would you then react?" I questioned with a warm smile. He replied, "It would change everything. I would react by trying to help them, and I would enjoy my job more."

The key word there was "enjoy".

When you change your filter to love and gratitude, you bring light and positivity to everyone else around you. Delight at the opportunity to help others. Only then, can you be joyful.

KEY SCRIPTURES

"Then God said, 'Let there be light'; and there was light. And God saw the light, that it was good; and God divided the light from the darkness. God called the light Day, and the darkness He called Night. So the evening and the morning were the first day." – Genesis 1:3-26

"Love suffers long and is kind; love does not envy; love does not parade itself, is not puffed up; does not behave rudely, does not seek its own, is not provoked, thinks no evil." - Corinthians 13:4-5

Chapter Nine Coaching Questions:

To experience more joy, what negatives in your life can you turn into positives, starting today?

Who can you pour out some love for?

My wife and I filmed our Christmas miracle family reunion on Christmas Eve. If you want your heart to be filled with joy, hope, and love, I invite you to watch this video. Click the QR Code to visit:

As a Special Operations combat veteran and someone who travels around two hundred days a year for work, I am no stranger to being away from home. After a fourteen-month combat deployment to Iraq, I didn't cry coming home. This was different because of the care from my nurses and the life-saving actions my wife took for me. After having overcome the fear of never seeing them again, I couldn't hold back.

Later I asked my wife how she felt when she saw me, and she said, both joyful and terrified. I was joyful to see me alive and terrified that I still wasn't better and ready to come home.

Chapter 10

Healing the Whole Person

I made it home, and it was joyous. When my mother showed up at my house, though, my wife's stress rose, and she rolled her eyes.

"Sean, she's your mother, so you deal with her."

Prior to this, the last time my wife and mother had hung out, I was traveling for project work. My mother had said something that made Monica feel judged, or demeaned, and it caused an argument. As mentioned in the beginning of the book, my mother was not the healthiest person mentally for most of her life. Yet my mother also has a strong desire to try and help others who are suffering from any sort of mental anguish. To a healthy person, her approach and advice may not be well-received. This combined with her insecurity around her relationships, caused by all the lost relationships throughout her childhood, led her to losing most, if not all, the family relationships she had.

My brothers and I would seldom talk to our mother. I would have an obligatory call when I could muster the strength. Others she cares deeply about like her sister, Aunt Carol, and her niece and nephew had all broken off their contact with her for years.

And for the last ten years of my life, I harbored a lot of resentment toward my mother. My wife and mother would often end up in heated arguments, like the one I mentioned above. As a result, my wife would take out her frustration on me. I didn't have the tools to fix the situation, and as a result I let it perpetuate. This led to greater frustration from my wife, in which I would place more blame on my mother. This was a cycle of sin that I always wished would go away, but other than to distance myself from my mom, I had no clue how to eliminate it. We as humans will try to avoid, or even destroy what we resent. I never wanted to destroy my Mom because people had been doing that to her most of her life, but avoiding her was my M.O.

Now, here was my 74-year-old mom, standing before me at my entrance foyer, carrying her oversized purse, tears in her eyes, happy to see her oldest son alive. I was standing there with my oxygen tank in tow, barely able to walk around my house at the time.

Suddenly, when I looked at her, for the first time in years I harbored no anger toward her. Whether it was a result of the bombardment of prayer, the near-death experience, or my brush with God: All the years of resentment toward my mother were washed clean from my soul. When I looked at my mother, I knew why she was here. God wanted her to enjoy the rest of her life, have a closer relationship with myself, my brothers, her sister, her niece, and the rest of her family. I didn't know how, but I knew her showing up at my house this day was going to be as much about helping her heal her relationships as it was about healing my body from covid.

Chapter 10: Healing the Whole Person

<u>The Roommate's Call</u>

My mother's plan was to drop in, stay one night, and head back to her roommate's house, where she was staying. My wife could tolerate this one night. All of the sudden, my Mom's phone rang; it was her roommate. Mom's roommate explained that she had family coming over, and now that Mom had been exposed to me, who was just getting over covid, the roommate wanted my Mom to stay away from their home for at least 5 days, per CDC guidelines. My mother had nowhere to go, and to me this was part of God's plan. She was meant to be here to help me heal, and, in turn, God would use me as a vessel to help her heal her relationships.

My wife's reaction was unfavorable to say the least, but after I calmed her down, I went to work. Over the next 5 days, my mother helped cook, clean, and ensure I had my medicine. While she helped my wife tend to me, I used the Word of God to help her. After several dozen very physically exhausting and highly emotional conversations by the end of her five days, she was on speaking terms with everyone in her family, including my wife.

I could tell both my mom and Monica were harboring resentment toward each other. I asked my wife, "Monica, what do you resent about my mom?"

Monica replied, "She is always judging me. She makes me feel that I'm never good enough for you or her. She's not healthy enough to give *me* advice on how to be a wife, a parent, or anything else."

"Mom, how do you feel about what Monica said?" I asked her.

My Mom, going on the defensive and coming from a place of insecurity, retorted, "Why am I on trial here? I just try to help Monica when she has problems. I don't judge her." I could hear hostility in her tone, and scripture from Ephesians popped into my head. I knew I had to take a stand for Monica and present her without blemish.

Ephesians 5: 25 – 27

Husbands, love your wives, even as Christ also loved the church, and gave himself for it;

26 That he might sanctify and cleanse it with the washing of water by the word,

27 That he might present it to himself a glorious church, not having spot, or wrinkle, or any such thing; but that it should be holy and without blemish.

"Mom, what you need to understand is that Monica saved my life. If it wasn't for her, I wouldn't be here right now. I will not tolerate any disrespect, abuse, or hostility toward her," I said sternly.

My mom fired back, minimizing Monica's dedication to me, and judging her in the process, "She should take care of you and try to save your life. She's your wife!"

Right then and there I knew it was time to help her realize what she had been doing to my wife, and likely others, her whole

Chapter 10: Healing the Whole Person

life. What I needed her to understand was that the word "should" focuses on an expectation based on an assumption. You can't use the word "should" without coming from a place of judgment.

"Mom, I want to thank you for coming over, and helping nurse me back to health this week. It meant a lot," I said warmly, and with pure authenticity.

Her demeanor went from angry to appreciative, "You're welcome son. I love you, and I was so scared I was going to lose you."

Then I gave her a dose of her verbiage and tone toward Monica, to see how she would react. I wanted to see if she would feel that being "shoulded" on was also judgment.

"Although, you SHOULD be here to help me because you're my mom." I used the same tone to describe her efforts as she used to describe Monica's.

Immediately, she put on her proverbial boxing gloves, "You know, that HURTS Sean. I have been doing your dishes, changing your oxygen tanks, cooking, and cleaning while you recovered, and now that's how you're going to treat me?"

I stood up, for the first time in hours. I wanted to show her how important what I was about to say was. "Being judged doesn't feel so good does it, Mom?" I continued, "I don't feel that way about you, or what you've done for me. In fact, I had no expectation that you would help me at all. That being said, you have come here, and given me a ton of time and effort, and I feel very grateful, just like I said earlier. I meant that. What you need to understand is how being judged makes you feel. Because every time you do that to others, now you know how and why they react the way they do."

Just like that, a Bible verse came to mind, one I don't recall reading, learning, or using in the past.

"Therefore, let us not judge one another anymore, but rather resolve this, not to put a stumbling block or a cause to fall in our brother's way." - Romans 14:13

I shared this verse with my mom and wife. I could see my wife's appreciation in that I had finally taken a stand for her, like a husband is called to do by God. I could see the understanding and empathy in my mother's eyes as tears began to roll out.

My mother choked back tears and spoke first, "Monica, I am so sorry for judging you. Sean's right in that I communicate this way. There's no excuse for it, but I want you to know that my entire life I have been criticized and judged by family, so it's been the only way I've learned to speak with others. It will not happen again. Will you please forgive me?"

Monica chose to forgive, but not forget. She is giving my mother grace and time so that their relationship can heal. No longer will I avoid my mother, trying to keep from further pain from resentment. As a result, my relationship with my mother and her relationship with everyone else around her is beginning to grow; and people are able to speak with her, without feeling judgment.

LESSON LEARNED

<u>Be Biblical</u>

I share this part of the story with you because there are several lessons to learn here. First, use the scripture as a guide to mend relationships. This 2000+ year old Book has all the answers you need to mend any broken relationship. In this case, the word helped me be a better husband for my wife. Helped me honor my mother. And helped me resolve family issues that went back decades, with one powerful conversation. Using the word of God, you can let go of pride, ego, and resentments and you will be happier. Everyone has someone in their family whom they wish they could love, but pride gets in the way. God gives you this amazing life, and all the amazing people in your life that you get to share the earth with are there for a reason. Love them and let go of resentment toward them so you can mend things. God wants you to experience His love, and the love of everyone in your family. But you can't accept the gift of love if you're holding on to the weight of resentment.

KEY SCRIPTURES

"Husbands, love your wives, even as Christ also loved the church, and gave himself for it; That he might sanctify and cleanse it with the washing of water by the word, That he might present it to himself a glorious church, not having spot, or wrinkle, or any such thing; but that it should be holy and without blemish." – Ephesians 5:25-27

"Therefore, let us not judge one another anymore, but rather resolve this, not to put a stumbling block or a cause to fall in our brother's way." – Romans 14:13

"Honour thy father and thy mother: that thy days may be long upon the land which the LORD thy God giveth thee." – Exodus 20:12

Chapter Ten Coaching Questions:

Who in your life can you seek to forgive, and forgive again?

What adversity are you struggling to face down without the word of God to guide you through?

Chapter 10: Healing the Whole Person

To see a pic of my mother caring for me during her week stay with my family after the hospital visit, click the QR Code and visit:

As the steroids continued to lower swelling and help me heal, my appetite grew. My wife, mother, and twelve-year-old daughter Ava cooked me four to six meals a day, and I was always hungry. It didn't take me long to put weight back on eating like that. Even weeks after leaving the hospital, I would struggle to stand up for too long and couldn't take stairs. Cooking my food was out of the question. Thankfully, my neighbors gave my family food and groceries to cook since we couldn't go to the store due to quarantine.

On top of that, I don't know what I would have done without those three ladies in my life, feeding me and caring for me all day and night. If you have a family member, friend, or family sick, please be there for them. It can make all the difference in their healing!

Chapter 11

The Endurance of Job

The other day we had a scare. I had a hypoxia episode where my O2 dropped to about 70, and later in the day, I coughed up blood. Surprisingly, I had no fear because I know my healing, and finishing this book, is part of God's perfect plan. That being said, since the doctors already found blood clots in my lungs and I am on a strict regimen of blood thinners, this was a big concern.

For Monica, this created a lot of stress, yet she stayed calm under the pressure. We called my primary care doctor who told Monica to call an ambulance immediately.

When the Rock Township Ambulance showed up at my house, it was the same paramedic who had taken me to the hospital over a week earlier, when I was knocking on death's door.

Rich, the young, thick bearded paramedic, walked into my room and boisterously shouted, "It *is* you again! You look GREAT!"

Rich shared his reasons for his enthusiasm and elaborated, "Man, when I saw your address come up, I was worried this was going to be a relapse or worse, that someone else in your family was going down the same road you had gone down. You were so sick when I took you to the hospital... You look so much better now! But let's get you checked out. What's going on?"

I showed Rich the cup with the blood I had coughed up as he listened to my chest and took my blood pressure.

Rich explained what was going on, "Your lungs have capillaries in them, and some of them are damaged by your immune response and are bleeding. For now, it's expected that this will happen."

Even though Rich gave my family confidence that I was going to be OK, the coughing up blood situation definitely created some anxiety for my family. I was out of the hospital; I was supposed to be "better".

Three months after my recovery, I still run out of breath walking up stairs. My joints still ache sometimes. There is still some COVID brain fog, as it takes me longer to recall some memories. And I am still taking blood thinners to remove and prevent the blood clots.

At the end of the day, part of this story reminds me of Job from the Bible.

Job was a very religious, successful, and wealthy man. God loved Job because Job feared God and shunned evil. Satan challenged God about Job. Satan believed if Job was stricken of all his belongings and his health that Job would turn away from God.

While Job's belongings, wealth, and health were stricken by Satan, Job did not turn away from God. Though he did challenge God directly and call him unjust.

When Job's friends heard about his afflictions, three of them came to be with him and support him in his struggle. Even though they started trying to figure out how Job had sinned so they could justify why Job was suffering, they were still there to support their friend.

I must say that I have had much more support than Job and would like to thank everyone.

God restores ALL

Glory to you, oh Lord, for through you all things are possible!

LESSON LEARNED

<u>Be Patient</u>

This can be the hardest lesson of all to learn. We live in a culture of instant gratification where we can have everything now, now, now! Well, it turns out, not everything. The road to recovery from COVID is a long one, particularly for those of us they call long-haulers. Many other diseases can take a long time to heal. My mother battled lymphatic cancer for years growing up. One of the bravest souls I know, one of my team member's wives, Meagan Kelly, has been battling cancer for well over a year, at the age of 27. While she was in remission, she and her husband Chas were blessed with a beautiful son. During her pregnancy, her cancer came back. I respect Meagan and Chas because, though they continue to battle the cancer, even in losing their health they are still happy because they spend more of their energy on the blessings they do have. When you lose your wealth, or worse your health, you can spend every waking moment worrying about what you've lost. And in the process, you will miss out on enjoying your life and won't appreciate the gifts you do have. Pray to God that He restores you, wrestle with God if you must, He wants that and He will listen to you. I know that God is faithful, and He does restore. It's now just a matter of waiting on His time and not mine.

KEY SCRIPTURE

"The Lord blessed the latter part of Job's life more than the former part. He had fourteen thousand sheep, six thousand camels, a thousand yoke of oxen and a thousand donkeys.

And he also had seven sons and three daughters. The first daughter he named Jemimah, the second Keziah and the third Keren-Happuch. Nowhere in all the land were there found women as beautiful as Job's daughters, and their father granted them an inheritance along with their brothers. After this, Job lived a hundred and forty years; he saw his children and their children to the fourth generation. And so Job died, an old man and full of years." – Job 42:12-17

Chapter 11: The Endurance of Job

Chapter Eleven Coaching Questions:

In what areas of your family, or business are you rushing to the result? If you chose to enjoy the journey instead, how would that make a positive impact on your life?

*WARNING, SLIGHTLY GRAPHIC: To check out Rich, my ambulance driver and I hanging out and celebrating that the blood I was coughing up was probably not lethal, scan the QR Code Here:

My initial reaction to coughing up blood was a brief feeling of dread. Immediately, dread was replaced with faith. Again, I asked myself, "Why would God keep you alive through the worst of it, just to kill you now?" The answer was, "He would not," and my fears were all but gone. I calmly explained to my wife that I was going to call an ambulance and that I was going to be OK. Unfortunately, Monica didn't have the confidence I did and had a brief panic attack. As a result, she decided to stay at her brother's house for a couple of days. This mental break helped take her mind off all the trauma.

Chapter 12

Coming Back to Life

How returning to life feels...

I am writing this chapter for the lives lost to the tragedy of post severe covid suicide. Among people recovering from severe covid, suicide rates are exceedingly high. Before my covid recovery experience and feeling the unimaginable pressure that comes with returning to the world after months of figuratively sitting on the bench, I could never have imagined why these suicide rates would be so high. Now, I understand where that level of depression may come from, and I want to offer solace and support to those battling through this emotional rut. If you are struggling with depression during your covid recovery, have a family member or friend who seems to be depressed, or the thought of returning to the world is causing you emotional pain, read on.

Growing up, I had a lot of social anxiety. Each day before heading to school, my stomach would be in knots. How will the other kids be today? Would the bully mess with me? How will my teachers treat me today? Oh no, I forgot to do my homework, my teacher is going to yell at me. What if my friend isn't in class today, who will I talk to? These thoughts would race through my head. The more time I had to think about these things, the worse these thoughts made me feel. The worse these thoughts made me feel, the more my mind would race. The longer time I was away from school, the more stress and anxiety I felt. Yet, as soon as I was there and in the mix with my class, things would get easier.

Nowadays, I am a public speaker, multiple business owner, and nationwide business coach and consultant. Doesn't sound like someone with social anxiety, right? In fact, an introverted friend recently called me a "God of extroversion." Which I did lovingly point out to him was blasphemy, but I digress. Regardless of what I now do on the outside, it's interesting to say that one thing this recovery experience has taught me about myself is that what happens on the inside hasn't changed much since I was a kid.

As the weeks of covid pneumonia recovery rolled on and turned into months, the thought of going back to work became more and more daunting. I had become very comfortable. I was enjoying my new routine. I could write whenever I wanted. My wife was making me eggs and sausage almost every day for breakfast. My team was shouldering almost all the burden of my company. Most of my clients were staying in touch and pouring out love and support for me. I was spending more quality time with my family than ever. I couldn't work out, so I was getting flabby. I was sleeping more than I ever had. Other than this pesky lung damage and pulmonary embolisms, life was pretty great.

At the same time, I had a deep sadness within me, and the social anxiety I have always battled and defeated by moving forward and jumping head first into the situations I feared most

Chapter 12: Coming Back to Life

was starting to dominate my thoughts. Horrible fears welled up from within. What if my clients decide they were better off while I was gone? What if I never get to spend time with my family like this again because of my business? What if I die on the road? How will I make up the missed project work income? What if I can't pay for all these medical bills? What if we can't keep paying salaries? What if I can't keep the non-profit going? What if I don't finish this book and get it published, people will think I'm a loser. What if I don't go back to work soon enough and I lose clients? What if I get sick again? What if I go back to work too soon and die because of it?

The emotional high I felt after my near-death, spiritual experience had worn off. The clock was ticking, getting closer and closer to getting back to the cold, harsh real world. I had been off work for over three months, and now I was feeling the mental consequences. My comfort zone had shrunk, my confidence was down, and I felt inadequate. As a result, I neglected some critical responsibilities. I stopped communicating with my editor and paused writing my book. In a couple convo's with clients, I came from a place of fear and scarcity instead of confidence and love. Instead of being present with my family, my mind was wondering or looking for ways out. Instead of filling my heart with faith and attending church mentally and physically, I was letting fear rule. By allowing the negativity I felt inside to consume me, I was allowing it to affect how I behave and communicate outside.

One thing we all have in common, as humans, is that we have a comfort zone. Imagine your comfort zone like a giant rubber band around you. When you go to do something outside your comfort zone, that band must stretch to reach that activity or action. As your comfort zone stretches, you likely feel stress and anxiety. If you're a human like me, and you have a brain that wants to stop at nothing to protect you, then you need to understand that your comfort zone is never static. When you feel stress or anxiety about something, it's your brain trying to keep you safe. It's identifying the things outside of your comfort zone as potential danger and telling you, "Oh no, you don't want to do that. You could get hurt. Stay on your couch, you can rest a little bit longer. It's safe HERE."

In reality, there is much more danger in staying inside that rubber band and allowing it to shrink to the point that it chokes us.

Another problem with our brains when trying to protect us, is that they default to the worst-case scenario. Notice the anxious thoughts I had as a kid? None of them were the positive thoughts. Notice the thoughts as an adult? Also, the worst-case scenarios. Our brains are creative and are really good at trying to get their way. Stay home. Stay safe.

"Okay, one more week," you tell yourself.

And in that week, your comfort zone shrinks even more. The fear and anxiety continue to build, and when you don't have the energy to continue to fear, it turns into depression. Maybe the financial or emotional hole becomes so deep, that you can no longer see a way out. You decide to turn to suicide. This is a true tragedy, and the thought of you, a perfect stranger to me, yet a child of God and a brother or sister in Christ taking your own life causes my very spirit to cry out in pain. While my situation may not be near as bad as yours, financially, health-wise, workwise, relationship-wise, I can certainly understand what you're going through. Now let me offer you a way out.

Now that you know your thoughts are simply defaulting to the worst-case scenario, and that your brain is trying to protect you from stretching your newly shrunken comfort zone, you have the knowledge to combat this situation.

The quality of your life is directly related to the questions you ask yourself. Be objective and ask this question, "What else might be possible?" Instead of focusing on the worst possible outcome, look at the exact opposite. It sounds like this:

What if my clients decide they were better off while I was gone?

What if my clients missed me so much while I was gone that they want extra coaching and services when I get back?

What if I never get to spend time with my family like this again because of my business?

What if this newfound appreciation for my time on this earth, and with my family, gives me the discipline it takes to make more time with my family?

What if I die on the road traveling for work?

What if I truly get to LIVE while experiencing life on the road traveling for work?

How will I make up lost income?

What if the lost income shows me who my most loyal clients are, and I give them more of me?

What if I can't pay for all these medical bills?

How great is it going to feel to pay these medical bills off! (I remember how making the last payment on my student loans felt—hah!)

What if we can't keep paying salaries?

What do I need to do, right now to get my financial ducks in a row?

What if I can't keep the new non-profit going?

It's okay to pace myself, and what small things can I do each day to keep momentum going on my non-profit?

What if I don't finish this book and get it published, people will think I'm a loser.

When I do get this book published, what if it becomes a best selling title?

What if I don't go back to work soon enough and I lose clients?

What will it mean for me, if the wrong clients I chose to work with in the past cancel our services and I get to find more of the RIGHT clients?

What if I get sick again?

What if God and the immune system he gave me protects me and I enjoy a healthy, illness-free life?

You see, for every fear and moment of anxiety, the exact polar and positive opposite is possible. In reality, the chips likely fall much closer to the mean/average than they will the polarizing ends of horrible and perfect outcomes. Remember to ask yourself, "What else is possible?" to give yourself some positive perspective.

Go to class!

The best way to stretch your comfort zone and get comfortable being uncomfortable is to simply stretch your comfort zone. Don't think, just DO. Before too long, you'll be sliding through the real-world situations with work, your social circle, and your finances with ease.

One thing I did was that I invited my team to come to my home office in St. Louis, for a team meeting. I gave workshops, and I asked them to give workshops. This was a great warm-up to getting back out in public speaking for me.

To get more comfortable in social settings, I reached out to some of the parents of my kindergarten daughter Emma's classmates, inviting them over for dinner. Even that created a little anxiety, but the great social interactions healed my soul and lifted my family's spirits. Not to mention, we made some new friends and deepened the bonds with them.

One of my team members, a hard-charging, lifelong learner by the name of Reid Richards, stretches his comfort zone by taking ice cold showers each morning. He says it makes everything he needs to do for the rest of his day easier.

If you're stressed about your finances, come up with a game plan. List out your essential bills, your ancillary bills, and your income. Come up with a plan to pay what's necessary when you can. Don't waste money on silly things you don't really need and when you get back to work, follow that plan. You, just like anyone, can generate more income in a lifetime than you can accumulate debt. Please remember, your life is worth much more than the sum of your debt.

Each night before sleep, I meditate to calm my mind and while deep breathing I focus intently on the work engagements scheduled for the next day. I imagine the people I get to see smiling, hugging me, thanking God that I am healthy and welcoming me back with open arms. I imagine the engagements playing out with me at peak performance. This lifts my spirits and boosts my confidence. After this type of meditation, I sleep very well.

Chapter 12: Coming Back to Life

When I first wake up, I might listen to a couple of upbeat, positive, faith-based gospel songs. It's said that people who listen to happy or positive music are less risk averse for a time after the song. Which means you'll be that much more ready to step back out into the real world.

As I prepare for work, I listen to audio books that teach powerful lessons, tell hope-filled stories, and lift my spirits. I avoid any news or negative media at all costs. A lesson from the late Zig Ziglar is that when you fill your mind with hope, faith, light, and love by planting seeds of optimism, those seeds will grow into fruit that makes many more seeds. That beautiful garden of positive thought will prevent the seeds of doubt from taking root and growing in your mind.

Talk about how you feel with the ones you love. I have found almost nothing more comforting than opening up to the people who rely on me most and getting vulnerable with them. One night I couldn't sleep because of the anxiety about returning to the real world. I knew my wife hadn't quite fallen asleep, so I told her that I was having trouble sleeping. I shared my feelings with Monica, something the old Sean would have never done. And she gave me great comfort when she said, "Your clients love working with you, they miss you, and they want you back. It's going to be amazing." Her words filled my heart with positivity.

Pray for peace. If you search for scripture about anxiety and stress, you will find solace in the Word. Then, take the Word and pray on it. Truly open your heart to Jesus, tell Him how you feel. Ask for the word of God to strengthen your spirit and renew your hope and faith.

LESSON LEARNED

<u>Be Courageous</u>

Negative thoughts (fear, pessimism, anxiety, etc.) keep us inside our comfort zones, rooted in inaction. This never made any situation better. It's important to look for the positive for every negative. When your mind jumps to worst-case scenarios, try to think of best-case scenarios (or, at least, most likely scenarios!) Find comfort in the Word.

I write this as I fly home from two weeks of coaching with clients in Indiana, Tennessee, Louisiana, and Ohio. The engagements went great, people smiled, people hugged me, I feel blessed to be back at work, and my comfort zone is stretching back out... But only now that I went back to class.

"Courage isn't lack of fear. It is acting in spite of it." – Mark Twain

Get back to class. It will be amazing! Or at least, not near as bad as you imagined. Because God is with you.

KEY SCRIPTURE

"In the multitude of my anxieties within me, Your comforts delight my soul." – Psalm 94:19

<u>Chapter Twelve Coaching Question:</u>

What action will you take to get your life back, regardless of the fear and anxiety that is trying to take hold?

Chapter 13

Another Epidemic: Unrealistic Self-Expectation

Not all plagues are physical and can be diagnosed in a hospital. Some are mental. There is a severe epidemic plaguing the business world. As I coach sales leaders throughout the automotive vertical across the country, I uncover this sinister and will-sapping plague time and time again. In fact, due to the frequency of this challenge, I've named this mindset U.S.E. which stands for "Unrealistic Self-Expectation." I define U.S.E. as when you hold yourself to standards that are impossible to meet or are out of your control. As a result, you become drained, frustrated, unmotivated, and unfulfilled when you hold yourself to standards that you wouldn't hold an employee to, your family to, or even your kids to!

When U.S.E. is uncovered, I ask the person I am coaching, "What is this mindset costing you?" Clients list unfulfillment at work, demotivation, an unhappy life at home, anxiety, lower confidence, lack of focus, activity paralysis, and even depression. What's worse is that while you make the mistake of holding yourself accountable to things out of your control, you can't hold yourself accountable to the things you can. As such, you won't take the right action, at the right time, in the right way that it takes to maximize your results.

Below is a coaching conversation transcript wherein I was able to shed light on this plague and help coach someone toward a cure. Before you read that, I want to share a traumatic war story that caused me to plummet into the abyss of U.S.E and share how this damaging mindset reared its ugly head in my career, in the worst possible way. Also, how overcoming these challenging, uncomfortable experiences, while unpleasant, has helped me to coach professionals around this challenge in the business world.

Mosul, Iraq, 2003. Our 3-vehicle convoy of HUMVEE's roared down a dusty Iraqi road heading toward the city where our PSYOP headquarters was located in Mosul. My three-person special operations team would travel this route through the sweltering Syrian desert weekly to meet with our commander and First Sergeant. The trip was always bittersweet. Sweet because we were excited at the chance to receive our mail and enjoy a slight change of scenery compared to our sweltering, fly-infested desert home to the south. On the other hand, the trip was bitter because the road was often littered with ambushes and improvised explosive devices.

I was the assistant team chief and turret gunner for my team, and I took my job seriously. From my vantage point in the turret, I would remain hypervigilant for the two-hour drive north. I was continually scanning the road ahead for debris that could be hiding a roadside bomb which would be set to detonate, destroy, maim, and kill as our non-up armored HUMVEE passed. On top of that, as each Iraqi car crept up behind our slow-moving convoy to pass us, I would switch the safety off my M249-

Chapter 13: Another Epidemic: Unrealistic Self-Expectation

SAW. The SAW was my thirty-pound belt-fed machine gun I would mount to my turret each time we would leave the wire, which could fire up to eight hundred rounds per minute toward an enemy.

As each car passed, I anxiously peered into their windows. The hyper-vigilance was partly because each car could be packed with a team of Mujahideen fighters. They would carry AK-47 fully automatic rifles ready to unload on us, or rocket-propelled grenades that were devastating. More so because our vinyl doors were no match for any of these munitions and, as such, I wanted to be ready to act in a split-second. Regardless of the threat, I decided that I wasn't going to lose someone on my team. I decided I wasn't going to lose anyone on our side for that matter. Unfortunately, while my decision was a noble one, with high intention, it was also a U.S.E. decision, and God had other plans.

As we rolled down a straight stretch of road, the searing hot wind whipping against my face, I noticed something in the deep ditch to the passenger side of the road. Consequently, thinking there was a potential ambush, I quickly rotated my turret and trained the sights of my machine gun on the potential target. As the object crested the drop off on the edge of the road and into my line of sight, I quickly realized it wasn't an ambush. Instead, it was, in fact, a tire and wheel well of an upturned civilian vehicle. A few seconds later, I noticed another vehicle in the ditch nearby. The crashed vehicles were white SUV's, Land Rovers, to be exact. These were the standard vehicle civilian contractors like the Army Core of Engineers drove. I yelled down the turret over the noisy diesel engine and extreme road noise caused by the aggressive HUMVEE tires to my driver, Specialist Beckman, and told him to pull off to the side of the road.

"Park near the vehicles but stay out of IED blast radius. Make sure we have a clear escape route ahead and watch out for buried explosives or wires!" I shouted.

As we parked just off the shoulder, our team chief Sgt Rutherford ordered 360-degree security from the rest of the convoy while we investigated the upturned and wrecked civilian vehicles.

What I saw while approaching the vehicles was unforgettable, and for these purposes, I won't go into detail. Know that inside the crashed vehicles, there were a group of ambushed civilians from coalition force countries. It appeared to me that Iraqi Mujahideen forces had pulled up alongside them and unloaded several magazines of AK47 into the driver's window and door. Consequently, almost all of them were murdered before the SUV even landed in the ditch. If there were any survivors, it didn't matter, because they also suffered wounds synonymous to AK-47 gunfire. These allies were Army Core of Engineers that had been carrying explosives which would be used to detonate Iraqi ordinance, for the demolition of unsafe structures. The enemy had decided to ambush them and take the powerful C4 explosives to create roadside bombs.

"That could have been us." and "How could someone take a life over something like this?" I remember thinking.

We frantically checked for survivors and found one. He had a faint pulse and was hardly breathing, but he was alive. We

Chapter 13: Another Epidemic: Unrealistic Self-Expectation

didn't have a medic with us, but we did have a "combat lifesaver," me. I had gone to the three-day course in preparation for the deployment. There I had learned to give an I.V., splint broken bones, and place a tourniquet on wounded limbs. My driver radioed for a medivac helicopter, which would likely take fifteen minutes to arrive at our location. All the while, I wanted to try and save this poor man from an untimely death with my feeble medic skills. Due to the lack of confidence in my ability, not knowing where even to start, fearing I would do more harm than good, and having no idea how long they had been in that ditch I was hesitant and unsure what to do. Together, my team and I pulled security and tried to help any way we could. Because of those circumstances, when the helicopter arrived to lift him off, I prayed that the men who had already died didn't have families at home. I prayed that the wounded lone survivor we found would make it through the night. Finally, I prayed I could forget what I had seen because I knew if I didn't forget, I wouldn't be the same again.

Later that day, we arrived at HQ, and in true military fashion, we had reporting to do around the incident. As if this detailed recount of the experience wasn't enough to reinforce the traumatic experience, a man with tear-soaked bags under his eyes and a British accent approached me and asked, "Are you the one who found my team?"

I solemnly said, "Yes, sir."

"Thank you..." He paused, trying to hold back tears, his voice beginning to crack. "None of them survived. Their families are going to be devastated." He grabbed my arm and began to cry. "You tried to save them, thank you."

All I could say was, "I'm so sorry."

None of my prayers had been answered, and there was no consoling him. Moreover, I had nothing good to say and no positive thoughts running through my head. All I could think was, "Sean, you failed. You should have been there sooner. You should have done something else. You should have done something more. You weren't a good enough combat lifesaver. His family is destroyed. You failed your objective to keep everyone safe."

These unrealistic self-expectations, or U.S.E., thoughts continued for years. This mindset was so hard to shake that it perpetuated into other areas of my life like business and family in the civilian world. It took me a long time to realize that this horrific encounter that I wouldn't wish on my worst enemy had rewired my brain to blame myself for things that were out of my control. I began holding myself accountable for events I didn't cause and had no control over.

St. Louis, MO, January 2012, Jeff Cash froze to death while walking home from a local tavern, and alcoholism had claimed his life, God rest his soul. It was excruciating because Jeff was like a brother to me. There were many reasons he and I were like brothers to each other. First, Jeff helped me get hired at the dealership I was now managing. He also helped me get on my feet by encouraging me to keep trying during my first rocky months

Chapter 13: Another Epidemic: Unrealistic Self-Expectation

selling cars. I appreciated the way Jeff would give me training after each customer interaction. Throughout the next 8 years, he taught me everything he knew about the car business. On top of that, Jeff trusted me to sell to his client base and ensured I always had fresh lists of prospects to call. Moreover, he helped me earn a promotion into finance and then was a massive advocate of moving me into a sales management role.

I had met Jeff about ten years earlier in the finance office when I had just gotten out of the Army. I was purchasing a car to replace the one I had just totaled on my way to work at Best Buy. During my transition from soldier to civilian, I was struggling financially. Partly, the struggle existed because the government had been providing my housing and food. Partly because my mother, who had been taking care of my finances during my two years of combat zone deployments, had been taking care of my bills. As a result, I became dependent on others taking care of business for me. To make matters worse, I had bought a house I couldn't afford during the subprime mortgage crisis on an A.R.M. loan, and I knocked up my fiancée. Oops!

That's why it was depressing when Jeff announced his divorce, worse when the heavy drinking became evident, and he began his long and steady decline. Jeff drank so much at times that he would pass out at work, and we would have to wake him up by pouring cold water on his head. The most challenging thing I ever had to do as a manager was to fire him. One of the many powerful lessons I had learned in the Army was that you couldn't put everyone's lives at risk over one person's self-interest. In this case, Jeff's lack of performance and moreover his inability to function at work was costing everyone steady paychecks, and it wasn't fair for the team. I let it go far too long and even had two salespeople quit because they couldn't work with Jeff in his capacity at that time. Regardless, once I finally mustered the courage to hold my friend, my automotive teacher, my career advocate accountable, he completely understood my stance. He thanked me, hugged me, and after he stumbled out of his finance office and I went to clean the remaining items from his office, I found dozens of empty vodka bottles.

As I bagged up the bottles, I thought to myself, "Sean, you failed. You should have seen this sooner. You should have done something else. You should have done something more. His family is destroyed. You failed your mission to keep everyone safe." It was like I was reliving the loss I had experienced in Iraq ten years earlier.

Shortly after that, fearing Jeff was going to drink himself to death, Doug and I tried to help Jeff. Doug was Jeff's best friend and my first manager in the car business. Doug was also the manager I replaced when he quit our dealership about two years prior. We decided to go over to Jeff's house to have a small intervention. When we arrived at his once lively house, I had memories of having dinner with Jeff and his wife. I remembered the sound of his two beautiful daughters laughing and playing, talking about Sponge Bob and chasing me around the house with Jeff's seldom used golf clubs. Now, it looked like a condemned forsaken house, and upon looking in the window, we saw Jeff sprawled out on the living room floor next to the couch where we used to play Tony Hawks pro skater on his PlayStation.

My heart raced, thinking he could be dead. Doug and I were able to get in through the unlocked front door and rushed to Jeff's side. What we saw caused a massive mix of emotion. It was appalling to see that Jeff had fallen on the floor and lay motionless surrounded by his unfinished French fries. Had something terrible happened? Was Jeff dead? Our dread intensified as soon as we noticed no less than fifteen empty two-gallon plastic jugs of vodka were dispersed across the floor, tables, and counters around his home. Finally, we felt relief to know that Jeff was alive and breathing!

Doug and I were feeling somewhat helpless to prevent Jeff from doing any further harm to himself. Thus, we decided to call the police and ask that they lock him up for his safety. Unfortunately, they couldn't do anything because he wasn't a threat to himself or others. We left multiple messages for AA groups, but it was evening, and they were all closed. We ended up telling the police that our dear friend was suicidal because that allowed him to be locked up for twenty-four hours. As you already know, it didn't save him.

The reason I share this story is that after Jeff died, the same self-defeating U.S.E. thoughts flooded my head. "Sean, you failed. You should have been there sooner. You should have done something else. You should have done something more. His family is destroyed. You failed in your mission to keep everyone safe." Again, I was reliving the loss I had experienced in Iraq ten years earlier.

You see, I had contracted the damaging mindset of unrealistic self-expectational thought, U.S.E. My brain had been wired by what had happened in my past. The first mistake I was making yet again were the demands on myself that weren't fair or realistic. The next error was the belief that I could control all these outcomes and situations. Again, I was telling myself, "No one can be killed on my watch." These expectations were fallacies, and I was setting myself up for failure. I didn't have control over Jeff's choices or his mental health. Heck, I could barely influence his behavior and had zero influence on the outcome. When you set expectations for yourself that you have no control over, that's utterly unfair to you!

Moreover, when things don't go your way, you blame yourself. As a result, we become jaded, unconfident, fearful, regretful, anxious, disengaged, or negative. We avoid new experiences which could potentially generate the same adverse outcomes. Giving yourself unrealistic expectations becomes a habit, and we begin to punish ourselves repeatedly. We should never hold ourselves accountable to circumstances that we can't influence or change.

This phenomenon occurs in war, and more frequently, in business. It is the equivalent of working for a manager who continually berates you and punishes you for something like lousy weather, or their favorite sports team losing a game. Except you are the boss, and you are treating yourself like crap! Does this sound fair to you? Does this sound familiar to you? This challenged mindset must be brought to the surface and addressed post haste. Because our brains operate in thinking patterns, each

Chapter 13: Another Epidemic: Unrealistic Self-Expectation

time you give yourself U.S.E., you perpetuate the cycle when you choose to allow yourself to set the wrong self-expectations.

What happens when you shift your mindset? How can you set realistic expectations for yourself? What actions and behaviors should you hold yourself accountable for? What does it feel like when you free yourself of these atrocious mindsets? What new actions will you take and what can it mean for you in business and sales?

For me to let go of U.S.E. I needed to permit myself to be human. I had to forgive myself for undesired outcomes in which I was involved but didn't have control over. I needed to let go of the outcome and focus on the process and only be accountable for that.

I don't have superpowers, and I'm not perfect. I can't predict the future, nor do I have mind control of others. As such, when I looked back and realized that I had taken action in all of these challenging events. These adverse outcomes were choices made by others, and I had given them a life raft to grab onto if they wanted it. Once I realized I would never hold others to these same ridiculous standards, I was able to let go.

Now, I make much better decisions around what I am responsible for, and as such, the actions I take are ultimately producing better results. What I want for you in reading this is to let go and begin to make great choices around what you do have control over. I want you to recognize that when you do have a negative outcome but took the right action at the right time and focused on the process and it still didn't work out, that's all you can do, and you need to forgive yourself. Unless you have a crystal ball and can predict the future, this may happen regardless of your process, and that's okay as well. Learn any lessons you can, adjust your process, and continue to take action around what you have control over. Give yourself expectations that you can meet. As such, you can set goals that you can accomplish and enjoy your work and life even more!

Now, let's apply this solution to your business. It doesn't matter if you're a company owner, a manager, or a salesperson, cure yourself of U.S.E. to improve your skills, take the right actions, and grow as a leader!

Here is a walkthrough of a recent coaching conversation where a sales professional I coached was suffering from U.S.E., starting with the last part of our discussion.

"What would make this conversation positively impactful for your career?" I thoughtfully asked. The coaching conversation had started with his greatest challenge.

"I need to get the enjoyment back in my career," he stated.

"Will you tell me more about that?" I asked.

This time he replied with much greater detail, "I'm anxious. I wake up in the middle of the night worrying about my sales. I just want to succeed, and ever since I changed companies, I haven't been as successful as I was before. It's wearing on me, and now when I deal with customers who aren't buyers, I get so frustrated. I left my last job because of these same problems, and I really like it here and want to stay. I'm not sure what to do. I'm just not happy with what I'm doing. I've thought that I might need a career change." I could hear the frustration in his voice.

Chapter 13: Another Epidemic: Unrealistic Self-Expectation

"Thank you for sharing your struggles with me." I was grateful for his willingness to be vulnerable because this deep level of understanding is where I can add the most value as a coach. "I want to ensure we address anything standing in the way of your career fulfillment in this conversation. Are you open to unpacking each of these challenges separately, then collaborating around an action plan to improve your situation?" These topics were deep, and I needed to know if he wanted me to be a shoulder to lean on for his problems or preferred to address these with actionable items through coaching. I believe that without action, coaching is just therapy.

With hesitation and pessimism in his voice, he replied, "That would be great, but I don't think it's possible, and even if it were, addressing this might not be a good idea"

"What would be a bad idea about helping you find less stress, more enjoyment, and success in your career?" I probed.

"Yes..." His initial confidence began to waver. "Well, maybe not." He paused, "I guess the problem is..." he paused again. "I think there are two versions of me. One version of me is stressed out all the time and sells a lot. The other version of me is laid back and isn't as successful."

After coaching many executives, high-achieving middle managers, and top producing salespeople who enjoy excellent results, I knew he was conning himself. I needed to coach him around this con. "Is it possible for someone to enjoy success without high levels of stress?" I probed.

"I think so, and I just have no clue how." He humbly laughed at his own opportunity to grow.

"How successful will you feel about this career, if you quit under these circumstances?" I asked another cost-based question aiming to learn if quitting would be an undesired outcome for him.

Tim quickly and confidently responded, "I would never want to quit under these circumstances, because I already did that once at my last job. Also, I like this company far too much to feel good about doing that again." Before I could respond Tim added, "That's a good point. If I don't address this, it doesn't matter if the stress helps me sell more or not, I'll quit again."

I asked Tim again, "Are you ready to unpack the challenges you've brought up and tackle each one in a vacuum?"

"Without a doubt!" he said excitedly.

"Other than success, stress caused by your inability to unplug from work, and unruly buyers, what other challenges should we address here?" I wanted to ensure we had clarity on where to begin.

"That's pretty much it. If we can tackle those, I think I can get to the level of success I want here," he verified.

Since words like success mean something different for everyone, I needed him to paint that picture. "First, I need to understand what success means to you. Can you help me understand what that looks like?"

He quickly threw out a result, "I would sell twenty cars a month and make about ten thousand dollars."

"In addition to the units and commission, what about that level of success is so important to you?" I asked.

"Mark, who recruited me, needs me to knock it out of the park. He told me that when he hired me, and I promised him I would do it. I just want to make him happy. Also, I don't want to go back now that I've already been to a certain point of success at my old dealership." He clearly felt like he was letting Mark, his hiring manager, and himself down.

"I respect you for wanting to please your new manager and exceed his expectations. How far off his expectations are you?" I questioned him further.

Silence.

"How many cars does he want you to sell, and what does he expect you to make each month?" I asked another way.

Chuckling softly, he said, "I don't know. He's never really given me a specific number."

"What is causing you to feel that you're not meeting your manager's expectations? Has he given you any sign that you're underperforming?" I wanted to know if there were non-verbal cues such as body language, or passive-aggressive behaviors coming from his manager that may indicate frustration.

"No, not at all."

I asked, "What assumptions might you be making about your manager's expectations of you?"

"All of them. I need to talk to the boss and find out, don't I?"

"Sounds like a great idea!" I allowed my enthusiasm regarding his idea to show. Now it was time to turn an idea into an action item or plan, "Are you willing to do that?"

"Absolutely. I'll do it right away." He declared.

As I took notes around his first commitment, I asked a follow-up question around his past performance, "Also, in your prime, how many cars were you selling at your old dealership?"

"My last full year at my old store, I sold about two hundred and fifty-five cars!" He proclaimed proudly.

I wanted to find out how far he had declined since joining this new team, "Now, how many cars per month are you selling?"

"I've been here for about four months. I had a rough first month, we were really slow, and I sold about thirteen. I told the dealership it was my fault for hiring me." He laughed "My second month was amazing, and I sold twenty-seven cars! The last couple of months have been pretty good. Selling about twenty." He finished there.

I jotted "U.S.E.?" in my notebook regarding the way he was potentially blaming himself for the dealership's lousy month, and I also began to do the math on his results. Next, I asked, "Ok, other than the company you work for, and your results, what else has changed?"

Silence.

"Have you been doing everything the right way? As in, are you following your processes, working as hard as you usually do, and being personally accountable?" I dug deeper.

"Well, it took me a while to get used to the new pricing system here. It's been such a cultural change from my old company. I had to learn a whole new way of doing business. I feel like I've got it down now, though." He stated.

Chapter 13: Another Epidemic: Unrealistic Self-Expectation

"Okay, great, thank you!" I said excitedly. I was excited because I now had the information I needed. I believed I had uncovered the puzzle pieces he was missing, The missing puzzle pieces were the ones I had, and that's where I can make an impact. I had to verify this before I attempted to add value, but there was still the matter of the customer frustration. "I think we are arriving at a point that I can help you with your greatest challenge. Before we do, what is it that you enjoy and dislike about your customer interactions as it relates to your career responsibilities?"

"I really like educating them, training and bettering people. When they are open to that sort of thing." I could hear the passion in his voice again. Then the spark faded as he explained the downside in detail, "Nowadays it seems customers always know what they want. They have done their homework and don't want to deal with a salesperson anymore. It's like they want to get in, get the best price, and get out. Some of them are only concerned about price and come across as downright rude. I don't think it's fair to be treated like that when they don't even know me."

I replied with another question, "What does a rude customer sound like?"

"They don't want help, won't let me ask them questions to help them, or teach them anything," he pointed out.

"It sounds like you have already identified your ideal customer. Someone who wants to learn, gain an education, and enjoy a two-way dialogue. Is that correct?"

"Absolutely."

"Also, it sounds to me like you have defined your brand in the automotive sales world. Something like #TheAutoEducator I help people learn about and find the perfect car for their families!" Ensuring we are aligned in his definition of his personal brand.

"Okay, this is almost creepy! At my last dealership, they used to call me the Car Professor!" He laughed.

"Have you chosen to use this brand to find, attract, and engage with customers to set expectations with and create your ideal customers?" I asked.

"I can't say that I have."

It was time for me to drop the coaching hammer and give him the missing puzzle pieces. Tim, like most professionals, have 97% of what it takes to achieve what they want most in their head. It's the 3% of puzzle pieces they don't have, that as a coach I need to uncover. In that way, each piece of information I share, every story I tell is a guaranteed value add. "It's time for me to add value... are you ready to grow as a person and a professional?" I confidently asked him.

"Please!" he said.

"First off, what would it mean for you if you could wait on customers who wanted to work with someone like you each and every time?" I asked, seeking to crystallize this new possibility further.

"It would mean the world to me," he said hopefully.

"What I want for you, is that you enjoy working with each customer that you choose to work with because they like buying cars from a knowledgeable salesperson such as yourself. I want

Chapter 13: Another Epidemic: Unrealistic Self-Expectation

the customers you work with to seek out and appreciate the level at which you educate your customers." I was recruiting him to the conversation because people choose a side within the first ten seconds of a conversation. I wanted to be candid, and this can cause people to become defensive, to ensure he knew the positive intent I wanted him to choose the side that would fight for him, his coach's' side. I stated bluntly, "Then choose to wait on those customers, and choose to walk away from the rest. Give the customers who wouldn't be enjoyable to sell to to someone else. If you were going to enact a process to screen customers and allow yourself to wait on customers that would positively impact your attitude and actions, what would that look like?"

"I would tell them how I sell cars upfront, the automotive educator, then ask them questions to see if they would want to work with me, and vice versa. I like the idea of defining my brand and process upfront. Maybe I could even talk to Mark about letting me learn service." He replied.

"Sounds like a great plan," I said.

Wanting to tackle the U.S.E. problem, I asked the following question, "Regarding your success levels... If you were my manager, would you ever get angry with me, browbeat me, think less of me, and treat me like a second rate citizen for not meeting expectations that you never gave me?"

"Of course not," he said.

"Is it possible to sell perfectly and still not make a sale?" I asked.

"Yes," He replied.

"Why?" I asked.

"Because you can't control all the customer's decisions, no matter how good you are in sales. No one can get everyone to buy," he wisely answered.

Time to drive the point home and show him that his success hadn't backslid near as much as he believed it had, "Now imagine you are my manager, and I was learning an entirely new process. I am your employee following that brand-new process and working my tail off. During that learning phase, I sold about 1.2 fewer cars per month. Would you be angry with me, browbeat me, think less of me, and treat me like a second-rate citizen for taking that much of a dip in results?"

"No, I wouldn't. Not at all."

"Then WHY are you doing that to yourself, Tim?" I asked.

He was quiet.

I raised my voice for maximum impact and memory retention, "Is there any value in browbeating yourself for results you have no control over if you are following the right process? Is anxiety, fear, and the result of quitting worth the payout of slightly better performance in the short term? Is it fair for you to think less of yourself, and believe your manager feels you aren't meeting expectations when you don't even know what expectations you're not meeting?"

"No, to all that," he replied.

"Tim, in reality, you're selling two cars less per month than you were before, while learning all this new stuff at a new dealership, and each month you're selling more! That's impressive!" I wanted him to start winning immediately.

"Thank you," Tim said with gratitude.

Chapter 13: Another Epidemic: Unrealistic Self-Expectation

"Are you willing to commit to waiting on more of the right customers, and create more of them knowing there are so many customers out there who would kill to work with a salesperson like you?" It was time to finalize his action plan.

"Yes. One hundred percent!" Tim replied.

"What mindsets and behaviors are going to be different from here on out, and what is your action plan after this conversation?"

With a chuckle and a sigh of relief, Tim said, "I am a dick of a boss to myself... First off, that's going to stop." The relief came as his mindset had shifted to a higher level of thinking, and his long-standing pent-up anxiety finally began to fade. "Looking back at my results, I'm happy with how I've done since the job change. I think I can do even more for my company when working with the right type of customers, or even in the right department. I think this conversation has ensured I'll be with my company longer and I can't wait to sit down with Mark, find out if he is happy with me or not, and discuss all this." He wrapped up with his action plan, "I am going to focus on what I can do and not stress out about the outcome. I'm going to tell my customers how I sell cars up front!"

As a result of our coaching conversation, Tim was now ready to hold himself accountable to activities that were in his control, instead of results that he could barely influence. Equally important, he was ready and willing to meet with his manager to clarify his leader's expectations in a dialogue instead of assuming he was failing to meet them. Tim gave himself credit for learning so much and not going backward as terribly as he had perceived after looking at factual data. Finally, this fantastic individual committed to begin selling in a way that aligns with his core values and beliefs. Doing so has ensured he creates more career fulfillment and avoids the feeling of hopelessness created when your environment, people around you, and behaviors aren't moving you toward what you want most in your career and in life.

LESSON LEARNED

<u>Be Kind to Yourself</u>

Covid was an opportunity to confront unrealistic self-expectations head on. At every turn, I had unrealistic self-expectations. I believed I could beat this thing in a couple of days. I believed I could take care of it myself and that I didn't need a hospital. I believed I could recover quickly without having to negotiate long-term side effects. I believed that I, and I alone, was the only one who could keep my business running with my constant presence and hard work.

One by one I had to admit the truth. It was going to take a while to recover, I needed expert care, I needed to have patience while I healed, and my team was totally capable of functioning without me.

There is a temptation to be hard on yourself regarding your past, your present, and even your future. The truth is, we all need to just take a deep breath and look at things more clearly.

We often hold ourselves to standards we would never try to impose on others. We know that it is important to be kind to others, but we rarely extend that grace to ourselves. Covid taught me to be kinder to myself.

KEY SCRIPTURES

"Who of you by worrying can add a single hour to your life?" – Luke 12:25 (NIV)

"And be ye kind one to another, tenderhearted, forgiving one another, even as God for Christ's sake hath forgiven you." – Ephesians 4:32 (KJV)

Chapter Thirteen Coaching Question:

What unrealistic expectations do you have for yourself, that you wouldn't dream of putting on other people?

To check out a picture of my Tactical PSYOP team in combat in Iraq, scan the QR Code and if you can figure out which one is me, you win a free hug:

In this picture, I am on the far right. My fantastic team and I spent months living out of our vehicle in the desert. At first, we went weeks without a shower. We were shot at, ambushed, and almost blown up multiple times. Yet, all the battles we faced were no comparison to the war I fought with covid.

Chapter 14

Spiritual Warfare:
We Wrestle Not with Flesh and Blood

I've been in a war in the traditional sense. Covid was another type of war, one the entire human race was involved in and many individuals were on the front line. Many have died from this war. However, there's another war that people don't often talk about and many don't even know exists. It's called a war of the spirit and it's every bit as real as those other wars.

After going through my near-death experience, being saved by Brittany Hibdon's spirit, cleansed with the prayers of thousands, and being touched by God, I have become extremely sensitive to this war that rages. Somehow, and I can't explain how, we as humans have a great impact on this battle between light and darkness, good and evil, faith and despair, heaven and hell. Also, the heavenly forces can ally with us giving us strength and power, and evil can attack us directly, afflicting us with rage, illness, and doubt.

Fight hate with love. Once you realize that the things and people you may "hate" actually make you better, you can begin to appreciate them. Appreciation is the path to love. Intensify that appreciation, acknowledge it regularly, amplify it more, and eventually it becomes love. Here are some things you probably don't love and may even hate! If you can turn these into love, it is profound, and you will be a happier person. There is, after all, a reason Jesus says, "Love thy enemies".

Here are fifteen things you probably don't love but might make you happier if you did!

1. Love your competition, they challenge you to be better.
2. Love your future failures, they can teach you the most valuable life lessons.
3. Love pain, it makes pleasure even better for you.
4. Love your customers, you wouldn't eat without them.
5. Love skeptics, they're giving you advanced notice of potential roadblocks.
6. Love discomfort, it means personal growth.
7. Love the flaws you see in others, they give you an opportunity to help them.
8. Love what you've lost, it helps you appreciate what you have and makes letting go in the future easier.
9. Love your past mistakes, they are the reason you are who you are.
10. Love change, it's the ONLY constant in our lives from day one, to the end.
11. Love being dismissed/ignored, it gives you freedom to be with the right people.
12. Love your fears, they help you get a clear picture of what you DO want to happen.
13. Love your anxiety, it's instinct giving you a chance to find acceptance.

14. Love differences in others, that's what makes you unique and necessary.
15. Love candor from others, they care enough about you to share your shortcomings to help you get better.

Which of these do you feel you need to embrace?

HOW TO IDENTIFY AND AVOID EVIL TRAPS

"I believe in a higher power. I think there is a God, but I don't read the Bible or go to Church. I think that's enough..." - Sean Kelley circa 2014 (After reading this far into the book, it may be hard to believe I said that, but I did.)

Have you ever said that? Do you currently believe this to be true? Let's dive into this and see if you still feel the same way after reading this.

The last time I drove a car before contracting COVID and ending up in the hospital was on Wednesday, December 1st. I was driving home from the airport and needed to stop and pick something up from the local grocery store. When I was in the checkout line, I observed a Mom and a Dad dealing with a very unruly child.

"I want candy and a soda!" The kid screamed at the top of his lungs.

"Stop yelling." The father said sharply.

"NO! Not 'til I get my candy and soda!" the child yelled again.

I cringed and felt for the parents in this predicament.

The parents were embarrassed and clearly frustrated. I'm sure this kid was just having a bad day. But let's pretend for a moment this was your kid. Let's also imagine that this child always does the exact opposite of what you tell them to do.

For most parents, it's fairly easy to identify ill behavior in a child. Yelling and temper tantrums in public places for instance. Touching a hot cookie sheet. Playing with electric sockets and forks. Hurting animals...etc. Even if you haven't read the Bible, you would probably agree with this Bible verse below, if you relate it to the Dad speaking to his child in my story above.

"A fool despises his father's instruction, But he who receives correction is prudent." – Proverbs 15:5

Imagine if every time you told your kid to not do something, they would throw a tantrum and do the exact opposite. I would imagine you would try changing the way you were parenting and disciplining quickly. If that didn't work, you would worry you have a sociopath, or a kid with some deep-seated issues that need to be addressed by a professional, quickly! What would happen if you allowed that behavior to perpetuate? How dangerous could that be for your kid, your family, and society?

As adults, what keeps us on the straight and narrow? Laws, made by man? Among all the people you have ever met in your life, who among them was perfect? I believe since we as humans are inherently imperfect, anything we make will inherently also have flaws.

Chapter 14: Spiritual Warfare: Not with Flesh and Blood

If Jesus Christ was indeed the son of God, then He would have been the last perfect being to walk the earth. Scripture is divine, and is absolute truth, and that claim is backed by miracles being fulfilled. Prophetic messages becoming a reality are one example. In the Bible, there are 270 prophecies tied directly to Jesus Christ that have been predicted in advance of the event, and authenticated later when they became true. Jesus affirmed the Bible as the "Word of God". Which means the process and writing within the Bible is, in fact, divine.

If this is the case, and you believe in a higher power, a Creator that made you and me, He would be your Father. Your true parent. What does the bible say about that? There are hundreds of verses calling God your Father.

"In this manner, therefore, pray: Our Father in heaven, Hallowed be Your name.
Your kingdom come. Your will be done On earth as it is in heaven." - Matthew 6:9-10

If God sent his son Jesus to us, and 270 prophecies involving Jesus are confirmed to be true, and prophecies that come true are miracles and that's a requirement to make it into the Bible, and Jesus affirmed that the Bible is the word of God, and God is our Father, and we believe per Matthew 6: 9-10 that we are supposed to follow His WILL here on earth as it is in heaven, and we would be a fool to not follow our Father's instruction, then that means the WORD of GOD is the ultimate instruction from our Father.

To ignore the word of God and just believe in a "higher power" is the equivalent of your child saying, "My father exists, but if I don't listen to or read his instructions or follow his rules, then they don't exist."

What does the Bible say about the Word of God?

"For the word of God is living and powerful, and sharper than any two-edged sword, piercing even to the division of soul and spirit, and of joints and marrow, and is a discerner of the thoughts and intents of the heart." – Hebrews 4:12

Sounds pretty important to me!

I believe that the scriptures within the Bible are the most POWERFUL tool we have to fight evil. It is the best way to identify evil, protect yourself from evil and lead your family to heaven. And it's because of this passage:

> *"Finally, my brethren, be strong in the Lord and in the power of His might. Put on the whole armor of God, that you may be able to stand against the wiles of the devil. For we do not wrestle against flesh and blood, but against principalities, against powers, against the rulers of the darkness of this age, against spiritual hosts of wickedness in the heavenly places. Therefore take up the whole armor of God, that you may be able to withstand in the evil day, and having done all,*

Chapter 14: Spiritual Warfare: Not with Flesh and Blood

> *to stand. Stand therefore, having girded your waist with truth, having put on the breastplate of righteousness, and having shod your feet with the preparation of the gospel of peace; above all, taking the shield of faith with which you will be able to quench all the fiery darts of the wicked one. And take the helmet of salvation, and the sword of the Spirit, which is the word of God; praying always with all prayer and supplication in the Spirit, being watchful to this end with all perseverance and supplication for all the saints— and for me, that utterance may be given to me, that I may open my mouth boldly to make known the mystery of the gospel, for which I am an ambassador in chains; that in it I may speak boldly, as I ought to speak." – Ephesians 6:10-20*

The word is truth, the word is your shield, the word is your sword, the word is righteous, the word is peace, the word is your preparation, the word is your salvation and your spirit. Thus, when you speak the Word, you can be bold because it is perfect. No evil, no lie, and no darkness can stand against the word of God, your Father's instruction.

So, this brings us back to the big question. How do you identify and avoid evil?

- Any human words and rhetoric that go against the Word of God are likely sinful.

- Any human actions, activities or behaviors that go against the Word of God are evil.
- Any human thoughts and attitudes that you have inside, that go against the Word of God, are the evil one making an attempt at persuading you to use evil words and take evil action.

Let's use a couple recent real-world examples from a very prominent political figure and contrast his words to the Word of God:

In an August 2019 press briefing, this political figure divided whites from blacks with blame, saying that racism was a "white man's problem visited on people of color." "White folks are the reason we have institutional racism," this person said.[1]

January 4th, 2022, the same politician divided vaccinated from unvaccinated with blame, saying that COVID-19 is a pandemic of the unvaccinated. "There is no excuse for anyone being unvaccinated," and then "This continues to be a pandemic of the unvaccinated."[2]

---

[1] Errin Haines and Juana Summers, "Racism in US is institutional, 'white man's problem'," https://apnews.com/article/election-2020-joe-biden-race-and-ethnicity-donald-trump-ap-top-news-88bd58010e75449eb5748499724df2f2 (accessed April 5, 2022).

[2] 'No Excuse for Anyone Being Unvaccinated,' CNBC Chicago, https://www.nbcchicago.com/news/national-inter-national/biden-

In addition, the WHO (World Health Organization) says that adverse reactions from the vaccine are likely underreported by up to 6 times. That means for every 1 adverse reaction reported, there are 6 that go unreported. The data the government is providing on the vaccine is questionable at best. That is one extremely valid REASON not to be confused with what this political figure is calling an "excuse" for not getting vaccinated. This makes the politicians statement not only judgmental and dividing, but also false.

How can we trace, track, and count every case of COVID that is randomly spread throughout our population, but we can't trace and track administered vaccines and accurately report on the adverse reactions caused by them?

Blame is judgment, judgment in the form of harsh words. Harsh words create anger, anger from one group to another creates division into two groups. Division is the opposite of unity, and the contrary scenario of peace, and love. Don't take my word for it, here is scripture, the Word of God, our Father on these items.

"A soft answer turns away wrath, But a harsh word stirs up anger." – Proverbs 15:1

"Endeavoring to keep the unity of the Spirit in the bond of peace." – Ephesians 4:3-6

---

no-excuse-for-anyone-being-unvaccinated/ 2721022/ (accessed April 5, 2022).

"Blessed are the peacemakers, For they shall be called sons of God." – Matthew 5:9

"And you, fathers, do not provoke your children to wrath, but bring them up in the training and admonition of the Lord." – Ephesians 6:4

"Fulfil ye my joy, that ye be likeminded, having the same love, being of one accord, of one mind." – Philippians 2:2

"Hatred stirreth up strifes: but love covereth all sins." – Provers 10:12

"Finally, brethren, farewell. Be perfect, be of good comfort, be of one mind, live in peace; and the God of love and peace shall be with you." – II Corinthians 13:11

Anyone or anything doing the opposite of the Word of God should be identified as sin, and evil is doing its work. In that way, we can avoid falling into the same trap. So, what do we do about the enemy? Do we become judgmental, divisive, and attack back in the same manner? Let's look at scripture on how to deal with evil and our enemies.

First, love them.

"Ye have heard that it hath been said, Thou shalt love thy neighbor, and hate thine enemy. But I say unto you, Love your enemies,

bless them that curse you, do good to them that hate you, and pray for them which despitefully use you, and persecute you;" – Matthew 5:43-44

Second, forgive them.

"But if ye forgive not men their trespasses, neither will your Father forgive your trespasses."
– Matthew 6:15

Third, pray for them.

"Confess your faults one to another, and pray one for another, that ye may be healed. The effectual fervent prayer of a righteous man availeth much." – James 5:16

Fourth, continue doing God's work.

"Let your light so shine before men, that they may see your good works, and glorify your Father which is in heaven." – Matthew 5:16

And finally, have FAITH that God will protect you against your enemies, because you are doing God's work.

"Though I walk in the midst of trouble, thou wilt revive me: thou shalt stretch forth thine hand against the wrath of mine enemies, and thy right hand shall save me." – Psalms 138:7

"No weapon that is formed against thee shall prosper; and every tongue that shall rise against thee in judgment thou shalt condemn. This is the heritage of the servants of the Lord, and their righteousness is of me, saith the Lord." – Isaiah 54:17

This is the 2000-year-old process for letting go of resentment. When you follow the Word and walk in Jesus's path in letting go of resentment, you free yourself. Imagine all the anger, frustration, and resentment you are holding onto is a 200 lb weight. How can you accept the gifts of the present with open arms, if you are holding onto all that hostility? We as humans will try to destroy what we resent. And we only have the capacity to focus on one thing at a time. If you focus on destroying your enemies, you won't put the energy you need to into building a better life, a better family, a better business, and you will miss out on your opportunity to bring God's kingdom to earth, as it is in heaven. Which is what gets you into heaven. Faith and fear cannot exist together, and by replacing your fear with faith, truly believing in your heart that God loves and protects you is the faith you need to eliminate your fears.

The scripture in the Bible is your ultimate guidepost to happiness, success, love, wealth, health on earth, and the ultimate true payout: eternal life after your body fails. Please do more than simply believe in a higher power because I want to be with you in heaven. God willing I am doing enough to make it in myself. Learn your Father's truth through His word, identify those who speak and do the opposite, and become self-aware enough to know when you are doing the opposite to identify and avoid evil traps.

LESSON LEARNED

<u>Be Wary</u>

Evil doesn't always dress up in horns and a pointy tale and wield a pitchfork. It can be subtle, insidious, even attractive. We must be constantly vigilant and hold everything we hear and read to a higher standard, *God's* standard.

KEY SCRIPTURE

"For we wrestle not against flesh and blood, but against principalities, against powers, against the rulers of the darkness of this world, against spiritual wickedness in high places." – Ephesians 6:12

Chapter 14 Coaching Questions:

Who do you often judge? How would replacing judgment with compassion enrich both of your lives?

When have you allowed words or actions of spite and anger to divide you from relationships God intended for you? How can you atone for those words and actions?

If you or your family has been harmed by covid and you are interested in volunteering or donating to the Cards for Covid cause, scan the QR code to visit:

https://cards4covid.org/donate/

Chapter 14: Spiritual Warfare: Not with Flesh and Blood   147

If you are a business professional or leader reading this, I would be both blessed and honored to speak for you at your business or upcoming event. If you would like to inquire about working together in that way, please scan the QR code so I can be YOUR visitor:

Appendix I

Sean Kelley's Personal COVID Survival Guide
Going to WAR Against My COVID

This is my personal COVID survival guide from my journaling throughout this process... Enjoy! And feel free to share with anyone stricken with the evil disease that is COVID.

After reading this if you or a loved one are sick and have any questions or need someone to pray with, text me at 314-323-8234. I will be here to support you.

> **DISCLAIMER:** *I am not a doctor, nor do I claim to be. This survival guide is based on my experience with COVID and COVID Pneumonia. Everyone's body, illness, and experience with COVID may be different. The information is current as of the date and time this is being written in late December 2021.*
>
> **BY READING THIS** *I may make no claim against the author, Sean Kelley, his companies, or any of his affiliates in reading this. I agree to hold Sean Kelley harmless of any indemnities that may arise from taking action as a result of*

the content herein. All content is for entertainment purposes only. In reading this I acknowledge understanding that Sean Kelley has not attended medical school and makes no representation of a doctor, nurse, or anyone else in the medical field. I also understand Sean does not represent or claim to represent any of the medicine or pharmaceutical companies or their products mentioned in this article. Please consult your doctors for tests and medical advice or support before taking any medication.

READ AND ACT AT YOUR OWN RISK.

<u>Finger Pulse Oximeter</u>

First, my wife decided to get me a finger Pulse Oximeter: I wear it on my finger, monitoring my blood oxygen levels and pulse. This is essential for knowing if/when you should go to the hospital and learning how your body is affected by movement/activity with COVID. You can walk into any drug store and get one or order online.

As long as you stay 90+ consistently, you're good! But, if you ever start dropping below 90, you should GO to the HOSPITAL. When blood oxygen levels drop too low, this is called hypoxia and would cause my heart rate to spike and caused me to pass out once.

Appendix I: Sean Kelley's Personal COVID Survival Guide

The day I decided to go to the hospital, I dropped to 60 when I stood up to urinate. I woke up on the floor in a puddle of pee. That's when I decided to take an ambulance ride!

Prevent Diarrhea

I needed Imodium since much of the medication I took caused diarrhea, especially since I got to bombard my system with antibiotics to prevent infections (which is likely with COVID pneumonia).

ALSO, to help my stomach heal and prevent as much diarrhea as possible, I took probiotics/yogurt/Metamucil and bananas. The probiotics and yogurt regiment will work to restore my stomach's flora, preparing it to be bombarded by antibiotics. The fiber in the Metamucil helped keep my stool solid. I did overdo the fiber and bananas, so you can end up with constipation which can be an issue that can cause hypoxia while going #2.

Spit Cup / Bottle

I always wanted to have a medium-sized bottle to spit mucus and blood into. Since this fluid is coming from my lungs, the hospital can test this liquid. Also, you want somewhere to store the fluid. (For nasal mucus, gently blow your nose.)

Nasal Spray / Nose Bleeds

I was on blood thinners and had Oxygen tanks blowing through my nose at 35 Liters for days. I found out that nose bleeds can be a real serious thing. Once I blew my nose real hard, and it took quite some time to stop the bleeding. So be gentle with your nose! I found out that Prescription Nasal spray soft tissue can be great for keeping my nose clean while being gentle with it!

Puke Bucket

COVID can cause stomach issues, and if one has a relatively easy gag reflex, they may want a puke bucket for deep coughing spells that may cause vomiting. I would tell that person to avoid vomiting, as it can take a LOT out of them in nutrients, hydration, and oxygen.

Combating the Cough

With COVID, I found coughing can aggravate my lungs and bronchial tubes to create additional swelling. Also, my chest can feel right, like there is a giant elastic band tightening around it. Finally, I had a coughing fit so bad that I pulled a neck muscle! The following advice will help you avoid these things and keep your cough manageable.

Appendix I: Sean Kelley's Personal COVID Survival Guide   153

- **Cough drops!** Yes, if one can find them, simple cough drops may ease pain and aggravation in one's chest and sooth your throat.
- **Vic's Vapo Rub or Icy Hot** - seems to help me open up airways sometimes.
- **Robitussin and Mucinex** - I quickly realized I wanted to be on a strict cough medicine regimen. I used about 5 - 6 bottles TOTAL over the month battle I had with COVID. On days I took this every 4 hours habitually, my quality of life was better.
- **Tesslon Pearls (Benzonatate 100MG)** - I was able to take these nifty little pills up to 3 times per day. They make a difference for me in coughs and chest discomfort. A doctor must prescribe it! They were a Godsend for me.
- **Nebulizers** - My wife got me these, and they are hooked up to a Phillips Respironics device that takes medicine, steams it, and allows you to breath it in.
- **Inhalers with Albuterol** - These can be used to treat your chest if you have asthma or bronchitis like I did.

<u>Sleep Apnea</u>

This can complicate severe COVID. I have centralized sleep apnea and, as a result, stop breathing in my sleep. Unfortunately, my BiPap (nighttime breathing device) is out for recall. After my 2nd or 3rd night at the hospital, my wife and mother reminded me to tell the doctor about it. The doctors put me on a BiPap with O2 hooked up which helped me get some serious sleep. If you have any type of sleep apnea diagnosed, make SURE you tell the doctors and try to get a BiPap.

What we Did To Attack the Virus

Monoclonal Antibody Treatment

As a child, I had pneumonia and asthma. As a result, I was considered a "high risk" COVID patient. Because of this, I was able to get the Monoclonal Antibody Treatment early in my infection. This treatment is highly recommended as the manufactured antibodies helped my immune system identify the COVID disease and attack it. Rumor has it that people with diabetes, obesity, immunocompromised people, in addition to asthmatics, transplant patients, and more, can be considered high risk and can easily qualify for life-saving treatment. Many doctors at hospitals have protocols that this treatment can only be given up to day 5, because after that its effectiveness is more marginal. So, seek this treatment out early in your COVID infection or you may have to visit a small family practitioner to get it. If you are in St. Louis and you want this treatment, call Heather Chaney at Madison Medical 573-783-4111 Option 7.

Ivermectin

Also, my wife was able to get me Ivermectin reasonably quickly from a local doctor. It tries to stop the virus in my body from replicating. If taken early on, it is believed to lessen the viral load on one's body.

Hydroxychloroquine

Monica also got me Hydroxychloroquine, which is similar to Ivermectin, in that it is supposed to limit the viral load. This medicine is taken by immunocompromised patients with Lupis and some other conditions. The FDA took this medicine off the EUA (Emergency Use Act) for COVID because they found it may lower the effectiveness of Remdesivir (used in hospitals to attack the virus). Also, when mixed with some medications, there is a risk of it creating abnormal heart rhythm. Studies were fairly inconclusive on the effectiveness of the medication. Though most of the studies were poorly done due the fact that the medicine was often given to more severe and older patients (people who needed more medication to survive) whose death rates are higher than younger, healthier patients. So, it's hard to say whether the medication is effective or not based on studies. I took this medicine for seven days before being admitted to the hospital, and as far as I know, I had no negative side effects.

I spoke with and listened to my doctors on ALL this stuff because I wanted to make sure the antibody treatment was okay if vaccinated, and I wanted to make sure all these treatments could work together for me. My wife chose to attack the COVID first instead of letting it have its way with me, but one of those was enough. But, in the end, I still needed to be hospitalized! Here's WHY:

COVID Attacked My Body in Three Ways

Organ swelling

This was identified with blood tests at the hospital. One surprising symptom I didn't expect was that I could barely walk. It felt like my legs and feet were battered and bruised from falling off a two-story building. Also, I couldn't get comfortable on my bed. No matter how I lay, I had back pain, joint pain, and muscle pain. This was my organs swelling. These are indicators I had extreme organ swelling and would be a great reason to go to the doctor immediately.

Doctors provided me with an anti-inflammatory medication called Baricitinib and IV steroids for organ swelling. These were critical to take to protect my organs from damage from swelling. Also, oxygen tanks at home or the hospital gave the swollen air sacks in my lungs life-saving oxygen. WARNING: all oxygen tanks are NOT created equally. I heard a story from a doctor about a patient who was welding oxygen tanks; he did more harm to his lungs than good. My wife found a credible medical company to deliver at-home oxygen!

Steroids are generally IV but can be inhalers, a potent anti-inflammatory. Steroids made me (and are still making me) have hot and cold flashes, make me uncomfortable, emotional, and irritable. Steroids can stay in my body for weeks after I leave the hospital. One would want to warn their family members that they might act a little wild and come across as demanding as they withdrawal from the drug.

Cytokines Storm

My immune system went haywire trying to attack the massive virus load and ended up attacking my lung tissue. Doctors identified it with fever and blood tests by testing white blood cell count. If your white blood cell count is too high, then your immune system could be ravaging your own lungs. When the virus load gets too high in a human body, people in their 30s and 40s are likely to have an extremely strong immune response.

For the Cytokines storm. It was about keeping my fever down and white blood cell count down. This prevented too much cellular damage from a white blood cell storm that went crazy and even began attacking my healthy cells.

Blood Clots

These are identified with CT scans, severe shortness of breath, severe chest pain, or physical evidence on the body (warm, red, painful areas of swelling). If one sees these areas, do NOT rub them. Get an X-Ray immediately. I had increased trouble breathing, more tightness in my chest, and some slight chest pain. When the nurse listened to my lungs, he couldn't hear sound in the lower lobes where the blood clots resided.

These were symptoms of blood clots, and the CT scan confirmed them. Larger clots would have increased these same symptoms. A blood test looking at your "D-Dimers" will find out if you are at risk for blood clots. Also, watch out for red, swollen, painful and warm areas in your legs. If you get those, you have clots in your legs. Do not rub them or apply pressure to them, because dislodging the clots into your blood stream can create dangerous complications. Instead, go straight to the doctor who will help you get them cleared up with the proper treatment.

They treated me with IV blood thinners for severe blood clots in an emergency. For ongoing treatment, while in the hospital, they gave me blood thinner shots injected daily into the fatty tissue in my stomach or blood thinner pills when I was an outpatient. I was prescribed blood thinner pills for weeks after COVID because I was identified as a high-risk PE (pulmonary embolism) or high-risk blood clot patient from some of the blood work and the fact that they found clotting in my lungs during my hospital stay.

I wanted to talk to my doctor about taking an aspirin proactively each day. I did this before the hospital, and I think it gave me a head start on the formation of my blood clots. Meaning they may not have been as bad. This is, of course, speculation because I have no way of knowing.

Remdesivir

In the hospital, they gave me Remdesivir. It's an anti-viral medicine that goes straight for the virus. They may do that if it gets rough. While you're on this, they monitored my blood for organ inflammation and blood clotting factors.

Oxygen

Oxygen Tanks

My wife could get Oxygen tanks delivered to our home. With COVID pneumonia, this was a lifesaver for me.

Concentrators

These plug into my wall and create Oxygen with some reaction. My doctor sent one of these to my house, and it produced 10 Liters of Oxygen. Unfortunately, this wasn't enough, so they sent me another and daisy-chained them together, so I had 20 Liters of Oxygen. This helped me breathe for a few more days before needing to go to the hospital.

Things that Cause Hypoxia

For me, with COVID pneumonia, I found specific activities that would cause hypoxia. (The dip in blood oxygen.) I learned to ensure my oxygen is on and cranked up for any of these activities. This will prevent a lot of pain!

- Changing body positions in bed
- Lying on either side
- Standing up
- Walking short distances
- Eating
- Defecating
- Stress / arguing
- Anxiety
- Any other physical exertion

Proning for Oxygen

Patients in respiratory distress can lie flat on their stomachs to make getting oxygen easier. This is called proning. I attempted to do a video of this in the hospital with nearly disastrous results! When I proned, I couldn't find my oxygen tube, and I went hypoxic. Ben came in and practically kicked my ass. It was well deserved, as I almost got a Darwin Award! Please don't be stupid like I was.

The Tail End of COVID

I have a TON of fluid leaving my lungs. A few days after I was discharged from the hospital, I started coughing up blood. We were worried because I had Micro PE blood clots in my lungs, so I called an ambulance. The paramedic came over, examined the blood in my mucus, and found out I was okay. Our lungs have tiny capillaries in them, and some of them were damaged and bleeding from the coughing, swelling, and white blood cells that attacked my lungs. Since I had COVID pneumonia, the cytokine storm, and organ swelling, I had to deal with coughing up some blood. I didn't freak out normally. IF there were copious amounts of blood like a deep cut or gash would produce, I was ready to call 911.

COVID Insomnia

I find it hard to sleep for more than two-hour periods. I wake up and just lie there and think or write. This is nice because it gives me time to meditate and gain clarity. I appreciate the time watching my family sleep peacefully as well. Sometimes, I wake up from coughing or fluid draining from my lungs. I nap as much as possible throughout the day to make up for my lack of sleep at night.

Secondary Infections

I was avoiding secondary infections! When I got out of the hospital, I wanted to travel the world and see ALL my friends and family. BAD idea! Catching a cold, flu, or COVID variant can be DEADLY while you're healing. My wife and mother made me stay the hell away from people. Smart ladies!

Antibiotics

Multiple pill forms may be prescribed; you can get these through the IV if you get really sick. I was given a cocktail of these things. I couldn't tell you which ones... all I know is that it was a lot.

Vitamins

I hear vitamin pills pull nutrients from existing food that I have already eaten. Regardless of my appetite or what stuff tastes like, I knew I NEEDED to EAT. After eating, taking a suite of vitamins helped me fight the infection and maintain a little energy.

Diet

You want to stay hydrated, but over-drinking water may wash out nutrients and can also add excess fluid to your lungs. With COVID, you may have a dry mouth and be extra thirsty; I trusted my body on this and drank as needed.

Eating tons of protein is essential. My body will have a lot of cells to replace and a lot of damage to heal. So, you will need a lot of lean protein! Eat all the eggs, sausage, chicken, fish, nuts, and more you can muster. Avoid a lot of carbs and sugars.

Avoid eating ANYTHING you could be allergic to. Also, sugars and carbs produce insulin which is an inflammatory agent. You'll want to avoid this because you're already fighting organ inflammation from COVID.

Vaccine

After COVID, you cannot get vaccinated or boosted for 90 days. I found out that while I was on the COVID Unit, about a dozen patients on my floor died, and many were intubated with ventilators. NONE of these COVID victims had gotten the vaccine. So, I would ask myself, would I rather have a rare chance to have long-lasting symptoms from the vaccine or a greater chance that I end up dead or in a difficult COVID life-threatening situation?

Prayer

LAST and NOT Least: Prayer! My wife posted online and asked EVERYONE to pray for me. This had a massive impact on my healing, spirit, and morale at the hospital. Also, most hospitals have chaplains that can see you. I would tell anyone at the hospital to do anything to get prayers!!! It's the difference-maker!

Appendix II

Hospitalization Packing List

This is my COVID Hospitalization packing list. It is for those who want to prepare for their battle with COVID and make their hospital stay more comfortable. Some of these things are common sense, others I will explain why I wanted them/used them. These items helped my stay be better, and the time started to fly by! BUT it took me a week to accumulate the things on this list and many I wish I had from day one. I make this list, so if and when someone else goes to the hospital for a COVID stay, they can bring this on day one, and as they heal, they will have everything they need to stay clean, alert, and safe while having a little fun and giving back to the team helping save them.

Picture of your family - You'll look at this for inspiration and love.

Cell phone – You will be doing a lot of calls and FaceTime!

Cell phone charger with extra long cable – The outlets can be far away sometimes.

Ear pods/earbuds – Rock out to music and/or listen to audiobooks.

Power Strip with 3-6-foot extension cord – Most hospital rooms don't have enough outlets.

Video game console – I wish I had had my X-Box. I could have hooked it up there!

Extra-long HDMI Cable – You'll need this to reach the little Television up high on the wall.

Laptop and/or tablet – Read, write, and surf the web. Also used to journal my COVID journey.

Disney+ subscription and phone app – So much great inspiration to watch (check out "One Strange Rock" hosted by Will Smith).

5 pairs of socks/underwear/T-shirts – Plan on a minimum of 5 days

3 - 5 Pairs pajama pants

5 Sweatshirts

1 Tennis shoes – Wear these when they wheel you around for a CT scan or X-rays

1 Pair of Slippers – Keep your feet warm.

1 Pair Flip-flops – For showers.

Fingernail file – Clippers can cut you, avoid cuts due to staph infection and blood thinners, use these to file your nails each day.

Hair clippers – Keeping your hair groomed feels good and gives you something to do.

Safety razors – Shave without cutting yourself; avoid cuts due to staph infection and blood thinners.

Hairbrush – Feels good to do your hair.

Toothbrush – The hospital toothbrushes just aren't that cool.

Toothpaste – Bring your favorite; trust me on this one.

Appendix II: Hospitalization Packing List

Shampoo/soap – The hospital all-in-one body wash shampoo leaves something to be desired...

Wet wipes - For when you get pee on yourself while trying to pee in a bottle at 3 a.m. while tangled in cords and cables, and other essential personal hygiene.

High protein snacks – Steroids make you very hungry, and the hospital nutrition department isn't open 24/7; protein repairs your lungs and cells. Avoid high sugar snacks; they raise your insulin which is an inflammatory agent.

Door Dash app – You can order non-hospital food AND, of course, buy your amazing doctors and nurses lunch to thank them.

Melatonin – A safe way to try to get some extra sleep in; it's hard to sleep with all the steroids, and the hourly check-ins/blood draws/blood pressure/temperature tests.

Thank You cards – To hand out to your doctors and nurses.

Get well cards – To give to doctors and nurses to hand out to patients that are struggling.

Deck of cards/Crossword puzzles – Something to do, you won't be leaving this one room for days, or even weeks.

Pillow – The hospital pillows can make you all sweaty, and the pillowcase seems to come off too easily.

Mini Fan w/speed controls – Steroids and Fevers give you hot flashes, cold flashes, cold sweats, and all sorts of other temperature-based body responses. One of these is a Godsend. (The hospital gave me one, but they only had one, and they had to dig for it. Bring your own.)

Appendix III

Healing Ourselves and Our Country

Since I began my battle with COVID, everyone's been asking me the same thing. Were you vaccinated? The answer is No.

Do I regret not getting the vaccine? The answer is No. But probably not for the reason you're thinking. At this point you might be thinking, "Sean doesn't regret not getting the vaccine because now he has natural immunity," but that's not the case.

The real reason I do not regret not getting the vaccine is that God wanted me to see this truth. Based on this book, as you will see, this was God's perfect plan, executed flawlessly. God needed me to almost die so that I could trust my employees to run the company when I wasn't there. God needed me to get sick so that I could see the truth about the medical professionals' dedication, selfless service, and love toward COVID patients. God needed me to have the most life-threatening type of COVID so that I could experience the myriad of COVID medications, treatments, side effects, and the testing that comes with them so I could speak the truth about them. God needed me to experience the mental anguish of the COVID victims who go onto ventilators and die firsthand, and the psychological trauma the nurses and doctors go through each day trying to save them. In this way, we were able to form Cards4COVID.org. This nonprofit is going to accomplish three things.

Cards4COVID

First, we are going to leverage the community of children in American schools who are depressed as hell right now. We are going to give them God-like purpose to give light, hope, and love to lonely COVID patients suffering in the hospitals. The children are going to create gifts, crafts, and get well cards and send them to a COVID unit. In this way, nurses will be able to hand them out to COVID patients to inspire hope in these lonely patients who can't have visitors, and often don't have families.

Second, we are going to provide mental health counseling and psychological support, and healing to the nurses and doctors who have PTSD. These nurses and doctors are extremely intelligent, and some have photographic memories. They might forget what they had for breakfast, but they often remember every patient they lose. This is a heavy burden to bear, and they won't have to shoulder it alone anymore.

Finally, cards4COVID.org will provide updated factual information and data cards to the public. These will provide accurate information on vaccine stats, medicines, hospital ratings, and COVID treatment options as things progress. Educating the public and forcing the government to create transparency aims to help the public indiscriminately be able to trust their medical professionals. In this way, the public will know COVID exists, and COVID patients will begin to say "yes" to the life-saving medicine treatments the doctors are offering them. They can choose life instead of dying in their bed because they don't

Appendix III: Healing Ourselves and Our Country

trust their doctors, like what happened to my dear friend, the late Brittany Hibdon.

My reasons for not getting the vaccine were many. I believed I have conditions that could put me at risk for potential vaccine adverse reactions. Also, the lack of data, and the rumors of changing data on the VEARS (Vaccine reporting website) made me nervous. Also, as aforementioned, the pushing of the vaccine by the government was a big turn off. I know many Americans share the same sentiment. I will outline the reasons I personally didn't get vaccinated and answer some other questions about the vaccine.

Reasons for so Much Push Back on the COVID Vaccines

My mentor and dear friend Chad Carden, known as the Architect of People, says, "When we fight things, when we push on things we can't control, the universe pushes back."

Americans value freedom, and most of us don't want to co-parent with the government. Americans do not want to be told where we can and can't travel based on if we're vaccinated or not. Americans do not want to be forced to wear masks that are questionably effective at best, and petri dishes for diseases when used ineffectively at worst. This is a study from 2018 done on surgical masks in extremely controlled environments: https://www.ncbi.nlm.nih.gov/pmc/articles/PMC6037910/

Can you imagine the type of germs a kid's mask in a school picks up, especially if they wear the same mask for an entire day? I'm no doctor, but based off the study, and common sense, I would recommend disposable KN95 masks only, and ensure the masks are changed every two hours. Otherwise, you may risk contracting other infections.

No different, when mandate advocates and government officials try to force the vaccine, they are pushing against something they cannot and will never control. They are creating more pushback than they can ever imagine, preventing vaccines from happening.

While I wouldn't consider myself a conspiracy theorist, I do try to consider all possibilities. One worst-case scenario possibility follows. As someone who went to the John F Kennedy Special Warfare training school for Psychological Operations, I did learn about how to influence target audiences. We learned to do this in the most credible of ways. That being said, we also learned about "Black PsyOp" in which enemies may use a "feint" or a "ruse" against us in battle.

In a trick like this, it's possible that the enemy knows the target audience enough that creating mistrust and spreading disinformation, first by hiding and manipulating data is a possibility. Adding the "mandate" and forced vaccinations from employers would certainly create a situation where fear-filled "sheeple" would take the vaccine, and God-fearing, constitution-following freedom-loving Americans who ask questions and notice inconsistencies would not. What would evil/communism have to lose at this point? The followers take the vaccine and live, and those who oppose tyranny and value our constitution die unvaccinated.

Appendix III: Healing Ourselves and Our Country

I pray each day that this is not the case. Yet make no mistake, evil is out there, the devil does exist, and there are dark forces at work attempting to influence us. This is, after all, spiritual warfare.

In the book of Revelation, the writer John points out that nations become beasts empowered by Satan when they exalt their own power and economic security as a false god, and then demand total allegiance.

This was Babylon in Daniel's day.

Then Persia.

Followed by Greece.

Then it was the Roman government in John's day.

Will we allow this to be the American government in our day?

The Judgment of the Vaccinated Toward the Unvaccinated

One of Satan's evil tactics is to create division, brother against brother, sister against sister, wife against husband. We are all ONE BODY, and Christ is our head. When we cut down each other, we are cutting down ourselves. When we sin against one another, because we are all connected, we are damaging our own bodies. It's no different than a cancer cell that forms, duplicates, and damages the entire body of a person. We are all equal under the constitution and in God's eyes. The sooner we start being mindful of each other, listening to one another, and seeking to understand, the better off we'll all be. The sooner we begin treating each other as brothers and sisters in Christ, and forgiving each other for transgressions, the sooner our body can heal. The spiritual warfare going on has done a lot of damage to the body, but it's nothing faith, love, prayer, and action can't fix.

Natural Immunity Versus Vaccine Immunity

Our bodies are amazing works of art. The way our immune systems work has been designed by our Lord and savior and has evolved, adapted, and strengthened over time. When a foreign invader like COVID infects us, our body takes snapshots of the virus's proteins and stores them in special immune system cells. These cells remain dormant inside our lymph nodes. These cells duplicate, and similar to the virus have mutations and variations around the virus proteins. This actually helps protect our body, not just from the original virus we had, but also its mutations and variants. If you've had COVID, you can get an antibody test, and if the antibody count is high enough, you can safely say you have natural immunity. As long as my count is over the recommended threshold, I do not plan on getting the vaccine. I will monitor this quarterly and as soon as my count drops below the mark, I will get vaccinated. Also, if a different strain comes out and a specific vaccine designed for that strain comes out, I will likely get that vaccine as well.

The Government Can Help Eliminate Division, Doubt, and Distortion

One of the best things our government can do to eliminate the division caused by Satan is providing transparent data. Elected officials' rhetoric can have a massive impact on people's behavior. One of the most divisive things I heard Democrats saying was when they were calling the vaccine "The Trump vaccine". How many "Trump haters" chose not to get the vaccine and died in the hospital of COVID because of those statements? If it was one, it was too many.

To eliminate distortion, the government needs actual case studies and hard data on all vaccinations and COVID treatments. A large portion of the US population is analytical statisticians. When they have factual data, they can use this information. Right now, there is too much misinformation, and not enough facts. People don't trust VEARS because of the inconsistent info and rumors that the data has been altered.

To eliminate doubt, the Government needs to make some changes to the HIPPA laws and give real nurses and doctors a voice. Almost each and every nurse and doctor I coach with strict confidence on their trauma of losing patients, or when helping them better empathize and engage with their patients to get more buy-in from patients around taking the medicine they need to live tells me everything we need to know about vaccinated versus unvaccinated patients.

Steve, the respiratory doctor told me, "I was in Oklahoma City during the initial outbreak, and the mortality rate was extremely high, well over ninety percent. The reason I chose to get the vaccine then was because one thing I noticed was many of the patients who were dying had A+ blood type, like me and you, Sean. So, I got the vaccine, and it's been two years of me working directly with COVID patients, and I haven't gotten the disease yet. I believe in the vaccine."

Doctor B said, "Social media and the internet don't make anyone smarter. There are a lot of fake videos out there of fake adverse reactions to the vaccine, created by people who don't care if others die. Also, remember this, because this is the largest medical trial in human history, in the billions, people are going to get the vaccine, and have medical conditions that would have happened regardless. Why wouldn't some people believe that the condition they came down with was caused by the vaccine? Of course, some people think they can take advantage of that, publicize their condition, blame it on the vaccine and attempt to sue."

Nurse Kathy told me, "Sean, none of the people dying in here are vaccinated."

Nurse Devann confided, "I wish my husband would take the vaccine. It terrifies me that he won't because I don't want to lose him if he gets COVID. I got the vaccine as soon as I could, and I've been in direct contact with COVID patients, and I haven't contracted the illness. Of the thousands of people I have had to put on a ventilator or have died since this started, none was vaccinated."

Appendix III: Healing Ourselves and Our Country

Nurse Suzie told me, "I respect people's freedom to choose to get the vaccine or not, but we had an unvaccinated nurse in our unit contract COVID and die. We've had a couple of vaccinated nurses get the disease and they were back to work and healthy in no time. I see it over and over, the vaccine saves people."

Why won't these testimonies be heard by the public? Why won't these nurses go on social media, and broadcast these messages to the world? Simple, they are fearful of the legal and career repercussions about speaking up due to violating company policies and HIPPA laws. The HIPPA laws are important for protecting human privacy, a right everyone should enjoy. But when nurses and doctors can't and won't share their experiences publicly, that leaves the evil one to create more propaganda to influence people to NOT get the shot, causing countless needless deaths.

Made in United States
North Haven, CT
14 July 2022